S0-AHS-208

Poetic Lives:
Coleridge

Poetic Lives:
Coleridge

Daniel Hahn

ET REMOTISSIMA PROPE

Poetic Lives
Published by Hesperus Press Limited
4 Rickett Street, London sw6 1ru
www.hesperuspress.com

First published by Hesperus Press Limited, 2009

Copyright © Daniel Hahn, 2009
The right of Daniel Hahn to be identified as the Author of the Work
has been asserted by him in accordance with the Copyright, Designs
and Patents Act 1988.

Designed and typeset by Fraser Muggeridge studio
Printed in Jordan by Al-Khayyam Printing Press

ISBN: 978-1-84391-301-6

All rights reserved. This book is sold subject to the condition that it shall not
be resold, lent, hired out or otherwise circulated without the express prior
consent of the publisher.

Contents

Samuel Taylor Coleridge died on 25th July, 1834, at James Gillman's house, no. 3 The Grove, Highgate. He was sixty-one years old. By the time of his death he had acquired an impressive collection of utterly devoted acolytes who would sit beside the great old man, to hear the sage share his visionary wisdom, and a horde of detractors who thought his writing overrated, his visions humbug and his best ideas plagiarised. He had attracted the harshest of criticism in the press, and the praise of some of the most eminent of his contemporaries. William Wordsworth, in the year of his friend's death, called him 'the most wonderful man that he had ever known'.

Coleridge's life was one of paradoxes, of tensions between conflicting impulses, between systems of belief, as he produced work that would attract absolute adoration and disdain in equal measure, as he engaged in painful struggles to reconcile irreconcilable forces and to find peace in a life that constantly troubled him. It was a tempestuous, sometimes a lonely life. It was rarely an easy one, and never ordinary. Coleridge wasn't an ordinary man.

Sweet scenes of childhood...

The old vicarage in Ottery St Mary was where it began. Ottery was – and is – a little market town on the Otter, in Devon. It was here that baby Samuel was born, at about eleven in the morning, on 21st October, 1772, to Ottery's vicar the Reverend John Coleridge and his wife Ann, and baptised on 30th December. He was named for his godfather, Samuel Taylor, but STC would never like the name (though he did always like 'STC').

Sam (as the family called him) was the youngest of the couple's ten children – all but one of them boys – and his place in the family was a mixture of indulgence (on the part of many surrounding adults) and bullying (by many children including some of his siblings – brother Frank especially). In one of the autobiographical letters that he would later write to his friend Thomas Poole, Coleridge would remember, 'My father was very fond of me, and I was my mother's darling: in consequence I was very miserable.'

He became quickly used to being in the company of his elders, and was by some accounts (including by his own) a very un-childlike sort of child. Entering the King's School in October 1778, Coleridge described himself as having 'all the simplicity, all the docility of the little child, but none of the child's habits. I never thought as a child, never had the language of a child.'

The Revd John was not only the local vicar but the local schoolmaster too, 'an exceedingly studious man, pious, of primitive manners, and of the most simple habits', who read the Bible to the local farm-workers (in Hebrew) and expected young Sam to follow him into the life of a country parson. His preternaturally adult child was a book-lover – who claimed to have read *Robinson Crusoe* by six – so very unlike his brother Frank with his preference for 'climbing, fighting, playing and robbing orchards'. After one particularly violent clash between the two, in late October 1779, young Sam ran away and spent the night shivering on the bank of the Otter, only being found the next morning. He would later ascribe some of his rheumatic troubles to this night of cold and general trauma.

His memories of childhood were not all bad, however; he was devoted to his sister Ann ('Nancy') and his brother George ('a man of the most reflective mind and elegant genius. He possesses learning in a greater degree than any of the family, excepting myself'), and to his father who encouraged him in his learning.

> … my father was fond of me, and used to take me on his knee and hold long conversations with me. I remember that at eight years old I walked with him one winter evening from a farmer's house, a mile from Ottery, and he told me the names of the stars and how Jupiter was a thousand times larger than our world, and that the other twinkling stars were suns that had worlds rolling round them; and when I came home he shewed me how they rolled round. I heard him with a profound delight and admiration: but without the least mixture of wonder or incredulity. For from my early reading of fairy tales and genii, etc. etc. – my mind had been habituated *to the Vast*…

On at least one occasion, Coleridge's father was moved to burn some of his son's more troubling books, but still the childhood years are remembered with some warmth when they appear at various places in STC's work, as in this poem written during his university days:

Sonnet
To the River Otter

Dear native Brook! wild Streamlet of the West!
How many various-fated years have past,
What happy and what mournful hours, since last
I skimm'd the smooth thin stone along thy breast,
Numbering its light leaps! yet so deep imprest
Sink the sweet scenes of childhood, that mine eyes
I never shut amid the sunny ray,
But straight with all their tints thy waters rise,
Thy crossing plank, thy marge with willows grey,
And bedded sand that vein'd with various dyes
Gleam'd through thy bright transparence! On my way,
Visions of Childhood! oft have ye beguil'd
Lone manhood's cares, yet waking fondest sighs:
Ah! that once more I were a careless Child!

John Coleridge was already in his fifties by the time his youngest son was born, and in 1781 (just before young Sam turned nine) he died suddenly, at three in the morning on 6th October, of a heart attack. His widow, faced with the daunting task of sustaining – and raising – her enormous family practically single-handed, quickly resolved to dispatch the youngest boy off to boarding-school. He was, after all, a smart child, a prodigious reader, precociously learned, and would surely do well. Ann Coleridge was ambitious, and expected good things of her son.

The arrangements were made by the boy's godfather Samuel Taylor and his mother's brother John Bowdon. After some wavering the school chosen was Christ's Hospital, then an establishment largely for the poor or orphaned, on the site of the Greyfriars, on Newgate Street in the City of London, a good 150 miles from the family home. It was a well-regarded institution, with over two centuries of history, that promised a good education and a thorough and responsible upbringing. No matter, perhaps, that the boy in question really, really did not want to go…

Christ's Hospital was also known as the Bluecoat School, for the distinctive uniforms worn by its boys – a uniform that identified the child as a charity case, and which caused young Coleridge some embarrassment – not least because his brothers made great show of trying to avoid being seen with him.

The environment at Christ's Hospital, under strict headmaster James Boyer, was far from warm, loving, or nurturing, and the nine-year-old Coleridge never quite thrived in it. He was odd, this reader, set apart from the other boys. He excelled intellectually, but was not happy. But he did forge friendships here – among those he met was Charles Lamb; this friendship would be the most enduring of his life.

Lamb would look back on his first schooldays meeting with Coleridge, and was struck – as all who met him would be throughout his life – by his speech, his animated manner and charisma as he spoke. This is Lamb's dazzled recollection:

> Come back into memory, like as thy wert in the day-spring of thy fancies, with hope like a fiery column before thee – the dark pillar not yet turned – Samuel Taylor Coleridge – Logician, Metaphysician, Bard! – How have I seen the casual passer through the Cloisters stand still, intranced with admiration (while he weighed the disproportion between the *speech* and the *garb* of the young Mirandula), to hear thee unfold, in thy deep and sweet intonations, the mysteries of Jamblichus, or Plotinus (for even in those years thou waxedst not pale at such philosophic draughts), or reciting Homer in his Greek, or Pindar – while the walls of the old Grey Friars re-echoed to the accents of the *inspired charity-boy!*

He would be known always as a great – and insistent – talker (with a Devon accent that persisted long after he'd left), a holder-forth of great presence and even greater stamina. William Hazlitt would write acidly (many years later):

> … to constitute good company a certain proportion of hearers and speakers is requisite. Coleridge makes good company for this reason. He immediately establishes the principle of the division of labour in this respect, wherever he comes. He takes his cue as speaker, and the rest of the party theirs as listeners… without any previous arrangement having been gone through.

Coleridge's own memories of Christ's Hospital would appear vividly in his poem 'Frost at Midnight', and in *Biographia Literaria*, where he would write:

> At school I enjoyed the inestimable advantage of a very sensible, though at the same time a very severe master. He early moulded my taste to the preference of Demosthenes to Cicero, of Homer and Theocritus to Virgil, and again of Virgil to Ovid. He habituated me to compare Lucretius (in such extracts as I then read), Terence and, above all, the chaster poems of Catullus not only with the Roman poets of the so-called silver and brazen ages but with even those of the Augustan era…

> At a very premature age, even before my fifteenth year, I had bewildered myself in metaphysicks and in theological controversy. Nothing else pleased me. History and particular facts lost all interest in my mind. Poetry (though for a school-boy of that age I was above par in English versification and had already produced two or three compositions which, I may venture to say without reference to my age, were somewhat above mediocrity, and which had

gained me more credit than the sound good sense of my old master was pleased with), poetry itself, yea novels and romances, became insipid to me...

Coleridge was expected to be a 'Grecian' – that is, a Classics student destined for Oxbridge; but his enthusiasms wavered (he had great capacity for enthusiasm); his brother Luke was studying at the London Hospital, and Coleridge spent time with him there nurturing ambitions of being a surgeon. Throughout his life he would be blessed – and cursed – by this butterfly temperament.

Occasionally his uncommon learning – which kept him so apart from his fellow students – served him well. Walking and daydreaming on the Strand one day his flailing arms caught a passer-by, and the young student explained apologetically that he'd been gesturing Leander swimming the Hellespont; the man was so impressed by this erudition in one so young that he gave Coleridge free access to a lending library on Kings Street; the lad was delighted, of course, gorging himself on books here, a hugely rich experience in contrast to the cold, Spartan, hungry life he had at school.

Though not pleased to be at school, Coleridge nonetheless returned home only rarely. One visit was made in the summer of 1789 (just as a revolution was being kick-started across the Channel); he described the approach to his familiar Devon landscape in 'Life':

Life

As late I journey'd o'er the extensive plain
   Where native Otter sports his scanty stream,
Musing in torpid woe a Sister's pain,
   The glorious prospect woke me from the dream.

At every step it widen'd to my sight –

Wood, Meadow, verdant Hill, and dreary Steep,
Following in quick succession of delight, –

Till all – at once – did my eye ravish'd sweep!

May this (I cried) my course through Life portray!
New scenes of Wisdom may each step display,

And Knowledge open as my days advance!
Till what time Death shall pour the undarken'd ray,

My eye shall dart thro' infinite expanse,
And thought suspended lie in Rapture's blissful trance.

.

Where dawns, with hope serene, a brighter day...

Destruction of the Bastile

I

Heard'st thou yon universal cry,
  And dost thou linger still on Gallia's shore?
Go, Tyranny! beneath some barbarous sky
  Thy terrors lost and ruin'd power deplore!
      What tho' through many a groaning age
      Was felt thy keen suspicious rage,
      Yet Freedom rous'd by fierce Disdain
      Has wildly broke thy triple chain,
And like the storm which Earth's deep entrails hide,
At length has burst its way and spread the ruins wide.

[Stanzas II and III are lost]

IV

In sighs their sickly breath was spent; each gleam
  Of Hope had ceas'd the long long day to cheer;
Or if delusive, in some flitting dream,
  It gave them to their friends and children dear –
      Awaked by lordly Insult's sound
      To all the doubled horrors round,

Oft shrunk they from Oppression's band
While Anguish rais'd the desperate hand
For silent death; or lost the mind's controll,
Thro' every burning vein would tides of Frenzy roll.

V

But cease, ye pitying bosoms, cease to bleed!
Such scenes no more demand the tear humane;
I see, I see! glad Liberty succeed
With every patriot virtue in her train!
And mark yon peasant's raptur'd eyes;
Secure he views his harvests rise;
No fetter vile the mind shall know,
And Eloquence shall fearless glow.
Yes! Liberty the soul of Life shall reign,
Shall throb in every pulse, shall flow thro' every vein!

VI

Shall France alone a Despot spurn?
Shall she alone, O Freedom, boast thy care?
Lo, round the standard Belgia's heroes burn,
Tho' Power's blood-stain'd streamers fire the air,
And wider yet thy influence spread,
Nor e'er recline thy weary head,
Till every land from pole to pole
Shall boast one independent soul!
And still, as erst, let favour'd Britain be
First ever of the first and freest of the free!

Coleridge remained at Christ's Hospital from 1782 until 1791. By the time he left he had been beaten various times for various minor transgressions (on at least one occasion recognising that the punishment was perfectly well deserved), he had been thrilled by the revolutionary news from Paris, and he had met the girl who would be his first love. The girl in question was one Mary Evans.

Mary Evans was sister to Tom Evans, a schoolmate of Coleridge's; Coleridge seems to have taken Mrs Evans, their mother, on as a sort of surrogate mother of his own, too – his relationship with Mrs Ann Coleridge had never been the warmest, and her banishing him to boarding school against his will had done it further damage, damage which would never really be repaired. His passion for Mary would blossom during his university years, lasting through those years and beyond.

Sonnet
On Quitting School for College

Farewell parental scenes! a sad farewell!
To you my grateful heart still fondly clings,
Tho' fluttering round on Fancy's burnish'd wings
Her tales of future Joy Hope loves to tell.
Adieu, adieu! ye much-lov'd cloisters pale!
Ah! would those happy days return again,
When 'neath your arches, free from every stain,
I heard of guilt and wonder'd at the tale!
Dear haunts! where oft my simple lays I sang,
Listening meanwhile the echoings of my feet,
Lingering I quit you, with as great a pang,
As when erewhile, my weeping childhood, torn
By early sorrow from my native seat,
Mingled its tears with hers – my widow'd Parent lorn.

Coleridge left school in August 1791, taking the night coach back home – but the home he found was a sad place indeed, with his brother Luke and his only sister Nancy having both lately died.

On Receiving an Account that
His Only Sister's Death Was Inevitable

The tear which mourn'd a brother's fate scarce dry –
Pain after pain, and woe succeeding woe –
Is my heart destin'd for another blow?
O my sweet sister! and must thou too die?
Ah! how has Disappointment pour'd the tear
O'er infant Hope destroy'd by early frost!
How are ye gone, whom most my soul held dear!
Scarce had I lov'd you ere I mourn'd you lost;
Say, is this hollow eye, this heartless pain,
Fated to rove thro' Life's wide cheerless plain –
Nor father, brother, sister meet its ken –
My woes, my joys unshared! Ah! long ere then
On me thy icy dart, stern Death, be prov'd; –
Better to die, than live and not be lov'd.

Saddened, Coleridge would not stay long at home, moving on to university in the autumn. That university would be Cambridge, and in particular Jesus College. Coleridge entered Jesus as a 'pensioner' in November 1791 (his entrance supported by an exhibition from his school promising £40 a year), matriculating the following spring – 31st March 1792.

He worked hard in his first year. In June 1792 he wrote an ode (in Greek) on the slave trade that won him the prestigious Browne Gold Medal for classical poetry. He would remember good times in the 'friendly cloysters, and the happy grove of quiet, ever honored Jesus College'.

After a summer vacation spent back home with the family at Ottery, year two was more of a challenge, as a number of problems began to beset Coleridge at university – problems which in slightly transmuted forms would be with him his whole life.

There were money troubles, with speedily growing debt. There was his persistent love for Mary Evans, with whom he continued to correspond – and who might have had feelings for him too, but whom he couldn't afford to marry. There were political upheavals distracting him from his study (not only domestic ones but foreign too – the fall-out from the still fresh French Revolution in particular) as he read his way through Thomas Paine, and Edmund Burke, and William Godwin, and became associated with some seditious fellow-Cantabridgians like the social reformer William Frend. There were, too, the beginnings of his problems with addiction – at this point, at university, it was alcohol to excess, which was troubling enough here, though as nothing compared to the abuses that would besiege his later years.

With these distractions, with the drinking, with – almost certainly – visits to prostitutes, too, the academics also suffered, inevitably. Things came to a head in the autumn of 1793. In November, the debts having got out of control, Coleridge finally went AWOL from Jesus College, resurfacing as one Silas Tomkyn Comberbache, lately enlisted in the 15th Light Dragoons.

(This, incidentally, after a last-ditch attempt to get himself out of trouble by winning the Irish lottery. He bought a ticket. He did not win. He did, at least, get a poem out of it: 'To Fortune, On Buying a Ticket in the Irish Lottery'.)

Enlisting was not, clearly, anything even vaguely close to being a good idea. Coleridge could not have been less suited to life in the dragoons. As though he needed to be marked out further from his fellows, he seemed unable to stop himself from dropping his classical learning into conversation – Euripides, Thucydides… He developed saddle-sores that made him unable to ride, so spent his time instead nursing a fellow recruit who had contracted smallpox. Eventually it fell to his brother George to rescue him, buying him out of his obligation, on the grounds of insanity, allowing for a (perhaps slightly abashed) return to Cambridge in April and a severe dressing-down from the Master.

The return to Cambridge was short-lived, however, and before the summer Coleridge was out again. He had fine plans that began with a proposed walking tour to north Wales with his friend and fellow undergraduate Joseph Hucks. The two young men stopped, first, in Oxford, where Coleridge made a friend whose impact on his life would be considerable (and not always – with the best of intentions – towards the good).

Robert Southey was an undergraduate at Balliol College, a republican poet and medical student. Coleridge's brief stop in Oxford turned into a rather long hiatus in the walking tour in order to allow the two newly met poets-to-be ample time to discuss the world and all its ills, and to come up with some solutions. It took several days.

The outcome of these late-night conversations between Coleridge and Southey was a scheme conceived by the two newly minted firm friends which they called 'Pantisocracy'. Essentially, their idea was to establish a commune in America – on the banks of the Susquehanna river in Pennsylvania – which would be an ideal society, composed initially of a dozen men and a dozen women, who would not succumb to the usual social vices of corruption, competitiveness, or any such evil.

On the Prospect of Establishing
a Pantisocracy in America

Whilst pale Anxiety, corrosive Care,
The tear of Woe, the gloom of sad Despair,
　　And deepen'd Anguish, generous bosoms rend; –
Whilst patriot souls their country's fate lament;
Whilst mad with rage demoniac, foul intent,
　　Embattled legions Despots vainly send
To arrest the immortal mind's expanding ray
　　Of everlasting Truth; – I other climes
Where dawns, with hope serene, a brighter day

Than e'er saw Albion in her happiest times,
With mental eye exulting now explore,
And soon with kindred minds shall haste to enjoy
(Free from the ills which here our peace destroy)
Content and Bliss on Transatlantic shore.

The early notions of Pantisocracy having been quickly sketched out, the walking tour could be resumed. Coleridge and Hucks moved on, then, towards north Wales, including a pause at an inn at Wrexham, where Coleridge was distressed to bump into Mary Evans; some days spent climbing various awkward Welsh mountains; and stopping at Ross-on-Wye, where the two friends stayed at the King's Arms and Coleridge wrote a poem:

Lines Written
at the King's Arms, Ross,
Formerly
the House of the 'Man of Ross'

Richer than Miser o'er his countless hoards,
Nobler than Kings, or king-polluted Lords,
Here dwelt the Man of Ross! O Traveller, hear!
Departed Merit claims a reverent tear.
Friend to the friendless, to the sick man health,
With generous joy he view'd his modest wealth;
He heard the widow's heaven-breath'd prayer of praise,
He mark'd the shelter'd orphan's tearful gaze,
Or where the sorrow-shrivell'd captive lay,
Pour'd the bright blaze of Freedom's noon-tide ray.
Beneath this roof if thy cheer'd moments pass,
Fill to the good man's name one grateful glass:
To higher zest shall Memory wake thy soul,
And Virtue mingle in the ennobled bowl.

But if, like me, through Life's distressful scene
Lonely and sad thy pilgrimage hath been;
And if thy breast with heart-sick anguish fraught,
Thou journeyest onward tempest-tossed in thought;
Here cheat thy cares! in generous visions melt,
And dream of goodness, thou hast never felt!

And then back to Bristol, to Southey and Pantisocracy.

The Pantisocracy scheme, pure and unworldly and idealistic though it was, would need some cold, hard cash to get it off the ground. (How vulgar.) And Coleridge did not have any (now, or really at any other time in his life). So, in an attempt to secure their preliminary fund, he and Southey gave a series of lectures in Bristol; and Coleridge published his first set of poems in *The Morning Post*, a series of sonnets appropriately enough addressed to a number of radical heroes like William Godwin and Edmund Burke, and other men and women he particularly admired.

To William Godwin, Author of 'Political Justice'

O form'd t'illume a sunless world forlorn,
As o'er the chill and dusky brow of Night,
In Finland's wintry skies the Mimic Morn
Electric pours a stream of rosy light,

Pleas'd I have mark'd OPPRESSION, terror-pale,
Since, thro' the windings of her dark machine,
Thy steady eye has shot its glances keen –
And bade th'All-lovely 'scenes at distance hail'.

Nor will I not thy holy guidance bless,
*   And hymn thee, GODWIN! with an ardent lay;*
*   For that thy voice, in Passion's stormy day,*
When wild I roam'd the bleak Heath of Distress,

Bade the bright form of Justice meet my way –
And told me that her name was HAPPINESS.

Burke

As late I lay in Slumber's shadowy vale,
*   With wetted cheek and in a mourner's guise,*
*   I saw the sainted form of FREEDOM rise:*
She spake! not sadder moans the autumnal gale.

'Great Son of Genius! sweet to me thy name,
*   Ere in an evil hour with alter'd voice*
*   Thou bad'st Oppression's hireling crew rejoice*
Blasting with wizard spell my laurell'd fame.

Yet never, BURKE! thou drank'st Corruption's bowl!
*   Thee stormy Pity and the cherish'd lure*
*   Of Pomp, and proud Precipitance of soul*
Wilder'd with meteor fires. Ah Spirit pure!

That Error's mist had left thy purgéd eye:
So might I clasp thee with a Mother's joy!'

There was rather a lot of literary production this Bristol autumn, in fact, most notably a collaboration with Southey on a verse drama, *The Fall of Robespierre*.

Bristol was also where the friends met the Fricker sisters, who seemed likely recruits to the first generation of Pantisocracy.

And the deal was struck – Southey would get Edith, Coleridge the slightly older Sara.

There was another significant acquaintance made now too – an idealistic tanner by the name of Thomas Poole, who lived not too far away from Bristol, at Nether Stowey. Poole shared Coleridge and Southey's vision for society, and was a useful sounding-board for their plans. The Pantisocratic duo had first met Poole on a trip they had made to visit a friend at Huntspill in August. This visit was memorable not only for the forming of this new friendship, but also because of an incident when Coleridge and Southey were locked in an attic by an innkeeper's wife, who thought they must surely be footpads. This was understandably an inconvenience to their trip, but, said Southey cheerily, 'Cheddar cliffs amply repaid us'.

There were two weeks in London, proselytising for Pantisocracy, especially at the Salutation and Cat tavern close to Christ's Hospital. Then late autumn 1794 was spent partly back at Cambridge, with Coleridge torn between passions – between Mary Evans, whom he still loved and who had lately written to him, and Sara Fricker, who was to be part of his and his friend's grand scheme and with whom – as Southey kept reminding him – he really ought to be keeping in touch in the interests of that plan…

Coleridge returned to London for Christmas, and decided to leave Cambridge once and for all, without taking a degree. He spent the Christmas holiday lodged at the Salutation and Cat, often drinking with his old school-friend Charles Lamb who lived nearby.

The first half of 1795 saw Coleridge settled back in Bristol. He read at the old Bristol Library on King Street, and lectured at the Assembly Rooms on Prince Street. His subjects were religion and politics – the latter was increasingly exercising him as he learned of the violence that had followed the French Revolution (of which there had been such high hopes).

Lodgings were found for Coleridge and Southey and a third Pantisocratic pioneer, George Burnett, on College Street, and it was shortly before leaving here in September that Coleridge paid a visit to the big elegant house at 7 Great George Street. Here, he was introduced to another promising young poet, by the name of William Wordsworth. Coleridge had heard good reports of William's poetry some years earlier, and had met his brother – Christopher Wordsworth – at Cambridge. The new friendship born from the meeting between William Wordsworth and Samuel Taylor Coleridge would transform the lives of both men, and – to put it no higher – would transform English poetry forever, too.

Not that Coleridge's own writing wasn't already making some progress before the union with Wordsworth; in August he had found himself a lovely cottage at Clevedon, and it was here on the 20th of that month that he wrote 'The Eolian Harp'. (The Eolian – or Aeolian – harp is a wind harp, the way in which it is played on by the wind making it an effective and popular metaphor for inspiration.) It is a poem which suggests a contentment, a tranquillity and a confidence that would later so often elude its author.

The Eolian Harp
Composed at Clevedon, Somersetshire

My pensive Sara! thy soft cheek reclined
Thus on mine arm, most soothing sweet it is
To sit beside our Cot, our Cot o'ergrown
With white-flower'd Jasmin, and the broad-leav'd Myrtle,
(Meet emblems they of Innocence and Love!)
And watch the clouds, that late were rich with light,
Slow saddening round, and mark the star of eve
Serenely brilliant (such should Wisdom be)

Shine opposite! How exquisite the scents
Snatch'd from yon bean-field! and the world so hush'd!
The stilly murmur of the distant Sea
Tells us of silence.

              And that simplest Lute,
Placed length-ways in the clasping casement, hark!
How by the desultory breeze caress'd,
Like some coy maid half-yielding to her lover,
It pours such sweet upbraiding, as must needs
Tempt to repeat the wrong! And now, its strings
Boldlier swept, the long sequacious notes
Over delicious surges sink and rise,
Such a soft floating witchery of sound
As twilight Elfins make, when they at eve
Voyage on gentle gales from Fairy-Land,
Where Melodies round honey-dropping flowers,
Footless and wild, like birds of Paradise,
Nor pause, nor perch, hovering on untam'd wing!
O! the one Life within us and abroad,
Which meets all motion and becomes its soul,
A light in sound, a sound-like power in light,
Rhythm in all thought, and joyance every where –
Methinks, it should have been impossible
Not to love all things in a world so fill'd;
Where the breeze warbles, and the mute still air
Is Music slumbering on her instrument.

And thus, my Love! as on the midway slope
Of yonder hill I stretch my limbs at noon,
Whilst through my half-clos'd eye-lids I behold
The sunbeams dance, like diamonds, on the main,
And tranquil muse upon tranquillity;
Full many a thought uncall'd and undetain'd,
And many idle flitting phantasies,

Traverse my indolent and passive brain,
As wild and various, as the random gales
That swell and flutter on this subject Lute!
And what if all of animated nature
Be but organic Harps diversely fram'd,
That tremble into thought, as o'er them sweeps
Plastic and vast, one intellectual breeze,
At once the Soul of each, and God of all?
But thy more serious eye a mild reproof
Darts, O belovéd Woman! nor such thoughts
Dim and unhallow'd dost thou not reject,
And biddest me walk humbly with my God.
Meek Daughter in the Family of Christ!
Well hast thou said and holily disprais'd
These shapings of the unregenerate mind;
Bubbles that glitter as they rise and break
On vain Philosophy's aye-babbling spring.
For never guiltless may I speak of him,
The Incomprehensible! save when with awe
I praise him, and with Faith that inly feels;
Who with his saving mercies healéd me,
A sinful and most miserable man,
Wilder'd and dark, and gave me to possess
Peace, and this Cot, and thee, heart-honour'd Maid!

Coleridge and Southey had lately befriended Joseph Cottle,
a publisher (and not a very good epic poet) who had a shop on
the corner of Bristol's High Street. Cottle was an early and
enthusiastic supporter of the poets' work, using his shop to sell
lecture tickets (indeed, Coleridge even sometimes gave the
shop's address as his own), and giving the promising young men
advances to allow them to marry.

And marry they did. Coleridge and Sara first, on 4th October,
at the church of St Mary Redcliffe – a church described by

Elizabeth I as the 'most famous parish church in England', and known in Coleridge's time for its more recent association with the tragic story of poet Thomas Chatterton.

The groom described himself, modestly, thus:

my face, unless when animated by immediate eloquence, expresses great sloth, and great, indeed, almost idiotic good nature. 'Tis a mere carcass of a face… my gait is awkward and the walk of the whole man indicates *indolence capable of energies*… I cannot breathe through my nose, so my mouth, with sensual thick lips, is almost always open. In conversation I am impassioned, and oppose what I deem error with an eagerness which is often mistaken for personal asperity; but I am ever so swallowed up in the *thing* that I perfectly forget my *opponent*. Such am I.

Southey and Edith married in the same church the following month. Southey must have been pleased with the way things were turning out, Pantisocracy-wise. After the wedding Coleridge took his new bride to the Clevedon house, where their married life seems to have begun rather happily. Happily enough, at least, that when Coleridge had to spend some time at Bristol away from home and Sara he wrote this poem:

Reflections on
Having Left a Place of Retirement

Low was our pretty Cot: our tallest Rose
Peep'd at the chamber-window. We could hear
At silent noon, and eve, and early morn,
The Sea's faint murmur. In the open air
Our Myrtles blossom'd; and across the porch
Thick Jasmins twined: the little landscape round
Was green and woody, and refresh'd the eye.

It was a spot which you might aptly call
The Valley of Seclusion! Once I saw
(Hallowing his Sabbath-day by quietness)
A wealthy son of Commerce saunter by,
Bristowa's citizen: methought, it calm'd
His thirst of idle gold, and made him muse
With wiser feelings: for he paus'd, and look'd
With a pleas'd sadness, and gaz'd all around,
Then eyed our Cottage, and gaz'd round again,
And sigh'd, and said, it was a Blessèd Place.
And we were bless'd. Oft with patient ear
Long-listening to the viewless sky-lark's note
(Viewless, or haply for a moment seen
Gleaming on sunny wings) in whisper'd tones
I've said to my Belovèd, 'Such, sweet Girl!
The inobtrusive song of Happiness,
Unearthly minstrelsy! then only heard
When the Soul seeks to hear; when all is hush'd,
And the Heart listens!'

                       But the time, when first
From that low Dell, steep up the stony Mount
I climb'd with perilous toil and reach'd the top,
Oh! what a goodly scene! Here the bleak mount,
The bare bleak mountain speckled thin with sheep;
Grey clouds, that shadowing spot the sunny fields;
And river, now with bushy rocks o'er-brow'd,
Now winding bright and full, with naked banks;
And seats, and lawns, the Abbey and the wood,
And cots, and hamlets, and faint city-spire;
The Channel there, the Islands and white sails,
Dim coasts, and cloud-like hills, and shoreless Ocean –
It seem'd like Omnipresence! God, methought,
Had built him there a Temple: the whole World
Seem'd imag'd in its vast circumference:

No wish *profan'd my overwhelméd heart.*
Blest hour! It was a luxury,– to be!

   Ah! quiet Dell! dear Cot, and Mount sublime!
I was constrain'd to quit you. Was it right,
While my unnumber'd brethren toil'd and bled,
That I should dream away the entrusted hours
On rose-leaf beds, pampering the coward heart
With feelings all too delicate for use?
Sweet is the tear that from some Howard's eye
Drops on the cheek of one he lifts from earth:
And he that works me good with unmov'd face,
Does it but half: he chills me while he aids,
My benefactor, not my brother man!
Yet even this, this cold beneficence
Praise, praise it, O my Soul! oft as thou scann'st
The sluggard Pity's vision-weaving tribe!
Who sigh for Wretchedness, yet shun the Wretched,
Nursing in some delicious solitude
Their slothful loves and dainty sympathies!
I therefore go, and join head, heart, and hand,
Active and firm, to fight the bloodless fight
Of Science, Freedom, and the Truth in Christ.

Yet oft when after honourable toil
Rests the tir'd mind, and waking loves to dream,
My spirit shall revisit thee, dear Cot!
Thy Jasmin and thy window-peeping Rose,
And Myrtles fearless of the mild sea-air.
And I shall sigh fond wishes – sweet Abode!
Ah! – had none greater! And that all had such!
It might be so – but the time is not yet.
Speed it, O Father! Let thy Kingdom come!

But the early burning enthusiasm for Pantisocracy had already begun to cool. There were arguments between Coleridge and Southey about money, and about politics, and Southey seemed to be more interested now in his new wife Edith. Which was all very well for him, but left poor Coleridge in an unfortunate position, having committed most inconveniently to that other sister. The foundations for the Coleridge marriage were hardly the most stable.

Keep the heart awake to Love and Beauty...

A big new project was beginning to occupy Coleridge's mind and his time around now. He had decided to launch a new journal of his own and others' writing, examining the current political situation and related issues such as libertarianism; it was to be called *The Watchman*. Its aim would be 'That all might know the Truth, and that the Truth might make us Free.' He spent some time in Bristol planning it (sitting with friends at the Rummer Tavern, just across the road from Southey's birthplace); and in January he went on a tour across the midlands and the north of England to sell a thousand subscriptions to finance the venture. Subscriptions were forthcoming (though not without a struggle), and by 1st March 1796 the first issue was ready to be launched. It would run to a modest ten issues, each printed eight days apart so as to avoid having to pay weekly stamp duty.

Finding Clevedon a little too isolated (Sara had fallen ill here in Coleridge's absence and had had to move back to the city), the Coleridges returned to Bristol, moving to Kingsdown. It was here, in September, that the couple's first child was born. Coleridge had lately become a great admirer of the materialist philosopher David Hartley; so the child was christened David Hartley Coleridge. (He would be known as just 'Hartley'.) The father was away for the birth, hearing the news while in Birmingham visiting his young friend (and potential student)

Charles Lloyd. Three sonnets followed hard upon the news, each increasing in tenderness:

Sonnet
On Receiving a Letter
Informing Me of the Birth of a Son

When they did greet me father, sudden awe
  Weigh'd down my spirit: I retired and knelt
  Seeking the throne of grace, but inly felt
No heavenly visitation upwards draw
My feeble mind, nor cheering ray impart.
  Ah me! before the Eternal Sire I brought
  Th'unquiet silence of confuséd thought
And shapeless feelings: my o'erwhelméd heart
Trembled, and vacant tears stream'd down my face.
And now once more, O Lord! to thee I bend,
  Lover of souls! and groan for future grace,
That ere my babe youth's perilous maze have trod,
  Thy overshadowing Spirit may descend,
  And he be born again, a child of God.

Sonnet
Composed on a Journey Homeward;
the Author Having Received Intelligence
of the Birth of a Son, Sept. 20 1796

Oft o'er my brain does that strange fancy roll
  Which makes the present (while the flash doth last)
  Seem a mere semblance of some unknown past,
Mixed with such feelings, as perplex the soul
Self-questioned in her sleep; and some have said
  We liv'd, ere yet this robe of flesh we wore.

O my sweet baby! when I reach my door,
If heavy looks should tell me thou art dead,
(As sometimes, through excess of hope, I fear)
I think that I should struggle to believe
    Thou wert a spirit, to this nether sphere
Sentenc'd for some more venial crime to grieve;
Did'st scream, then spring to meet Heaven's quick reprieve,
    While we wept idly o'er thy little bier!

Sonnet
To A Friend Who Asked,
How I Felt When the Nurse First Presented
My Infant to Me

Charles! my slow heart was only sad, when first
    I scann'd that face of feeble infancy:
For dimly on my thoughtful spirit burst
    All I had been, and all my child might be!
But when I saw it on its mother's arm,
    And hanging at her bosom (she the while
    Bent o'er its features with a tearful smile)
Then I was thrill'd and melted, and most warm
Impress'd a father's kiss: and all beguil'd
    Of dark remembrance and presageful fear,
    I seem'd to see an angel-form appear –
'Twas even thine, belovéd woman mild!
    So for the mother's sake the child was dear,
And dearer was the mother for the child.

Coleridge's admiration for David Hartley found its way into the
other significant arrival to the Coleridge household this spring.
April had seen the publication in Bristol (by Cottle) of his *Poems
on Various Subjects*, fifty-one pieces in all, which included 'The

Eolian Harp', his 'Monody on the Death of Chatterton', and 'Religious Musings', a 'desultory poem' which included some enthusiasm about David Hartley. Certain of the poems in the collection elicited praise – rather mild praise, but praise nonetheless.

Here are the beginning and ending of 'Chatterton', a poem begun years earlier when Coleridge was still at school, and which (unusually) he continued to revise almost his whole life:

from
Monody on the Death of Chatterton

O what a wonder seems the fear of death,
Seeing how gladly we all sink to sleep,
Babes, Children, Youths, and Men,
Night following night for threescore years and ten!
But doubly strange, where life is but a breath
To sigh and pant with, up Want's rugged steep.

Away, Grim Phantom! Scorpion King, away!
Reserve thy terrors and thy stings display
For coward Wealth and Guilt in robes of State!
Lo! by the grave I stand of one, for whom
A prodigal Nature and a niggard Doom
(That all bestowing, this withholding all)
Made each chance knell from distant spire or dome
Sound like a seeking Mother's anxious call,
Return, poor Child! Home, weary Truant, home!

Thee, Chatterton! these unblest stones protect
From want, and the bleak freezings of neglect.
Too long before the vexing Storm-blast driven
Here hast thou found repose! beneath this sod!
Thou! O vain word! thou dwell'st not with the clod!
Amid the shining Host of the Forgiven

Thou at the throne of mercy and thy God
The triumph of redeeming Love dost hymn
(Believe it, O my Soul!) to harps of Seraphim.

Yet oft, perforce ('tis suffering Nature's call),
I weep that heaven-born Genius so should fall;
And oft, in Fancy's saddest hour, my soul
Averted shudders at the poison'd bowl.
Now groans my sickening heart, as still I view
    Thy corse of livid hue;
Now Indignation checks the feeble sigh,
Or flashes through the tear that glistens in my eye!

[…]

Hence, gloomy thoughts! no more my soul shall dwell
On joys that were! no more endure to weigh
The shame and anguish of the evil day,
Wisely forgetful! O'er the ocean swell
Sublime of Hope I seek the cottag'd dell
Where Virtue calm with careless step may stray;
And, dancing to the moon-light roundelay,
The wizard Passions weave an holy spell!

O Chatterton! that thou wert yet alive!
Sure thou would'st spread the canvass to the gale,
And love with us the tinkling team to drive
O'er peaceful Freedom's undivided dale;
And we, at sober eve, would round thee throng,
Would hang, enraptur'd, on thy stately song,
And greet with smiles the young-eyed Poesy
All deftly mask'd as hoar Antiquity.

Alas, vain Phantasies! the fleeting brood
Of Woe self-solac'd in her dreamy mood!

Yet will I love to follow the sweet dream,
Where Susquehannah pours his untamed stream;
And on some hill, whose forest-frowning side
Waves o'er the murmurs of his calmer tide,
Will raise a solemn Cenotaph to thee,
Sweet Harper of time-shrouded Minstrelsy!
And there, sooth'd sadly by the dirgeful wind,
Muse on the sore ills I had left behind.

In addition to the writing and lecturing, Coleridge was now developing another strand of work, as a preacher. At this point in his life his confidence in his Unitarian faith was at its most firm; and when he tried preaching he found that he was very good at it, at one point even considering entering the Unitarian ministry as a viable career.

The engaging new work, the new baby, the collection of poems – these were not enough to keep Coleridge's spirits up, however; he began at this time to lapse into a disconsolate mood, added to a certain discomfort he felt from a variety of health issues. In order to alleviate the pain he was suffering due to (in particular) terrible neuralgia, he began to take doses of laudanum – for medicinal purposes only, at least at first. Laudanum (that is, opium taken in alcohol) was in the late eighteenth century a perfectly common pain-reliever, in no way stigmatised, and – though this was not well understood – highly addictive. Coleridge would always maintain that his opium-taking was never for pleasure, never recreational – that the only pleasure he took from it was the absence of pain it allowed him; but this, of course, is no bar to the development of an addiction.

The family needed a change, and a move away from Bristol might help. The friendly Thomas Poole was pressed into service to help them to find a new home close to his own on the Quantock hills in Somerset. He looked for a cottage first at nearby Adscombe, before finding one in Nether Stowey itself, immediately next door to Poole's own home, on Lime Street. It was a small thatched cottage, rather unimpressive, and Poole himself did not think much of it; but Coleridge was keen to move and Poole completed the purchase on his friend's behalf. Coleridge, Sara and baby Hartley had moved in before the year was done. Today it is 'Coleridge Cottage', and a popular place of pilgrimage to even the most amateur Coleridgean.

The late spring and early summer of 1797 at Stowey are a significant milestone in Coleridge's life – in terms of his work perhaps the most important yet – for two reasons. First, it was now that the brief acquaintance made of Wordsworth the previous year developed into a passionate, important friendship; and second, it marked the beginning of his *annus mirabilis* as a poet, a year that saw an extraordinary number of his finest and most enduring works burst from him, one after another, from his agile, fertile, sometimes febrile brain onto the page. 'The Rime of the Ancient Mariner', 'Kubla Khan', 'Frost at Midnight', 'This Lime-Tree Bower My Prison', 'Fears in Solitude', 'The Nightingale', 'France: An Ode', the first part of 'Christabel' and more, were all the product of the period between summer 1797 and summer 1798. (That the beginning of this period coincided with the sudden burst of friendship between Coleridge and Wordsworth is no coincidence, of course.)

Coleridge had spent the spring working on a tragedy, *Osorio*, and poetry that included this piece, to his brother, written on 26th May; Southey called it 'one of the most beautiful poems I ever read'.

To the Rev. George Coleridge

A blessèd lot hath he, who having passed
His youth and early manhood in the stir
And turmoil of the world, retreats at length,
With cares that move, not agitate the heart,
To the same dwelling where his father dwelt;
And haply views his tottering little ones
Embrace those agèd knees and climb that lap,
On which first kneeling his own infancy
Lisp'd its brief prayer. Such, O my earliest Friend!
Thy lot, and such thy brothers too enjoy.
At distance did ye climb Life's upland road,
Yet cheer'd and cheering: now fraternal love
Hath drawn you to one centre. Be your days
Holy, and blest and blessing may ye live!

To me the Eternal Wisdom hath dispens'd
A different fortune and more different mind –
Me from the spot where first I sprang to light
Too soon transplanted, ere my soul had fix'd
Its first domestic loves; and hence through life
Chasing chance-started friendships. A brief while
Some have preserv'd me from life's pelting ills;
But, like a tree with leaves of feeble stem,
If the clouds lasted, and a sudden breeze
Ruffled the boughs, they on my head at once
Dropped the collected shower; and some most false,
False and fair-foliag'd as the Manchineel,
Have tempted me to slumber in their shade
E'en mid the storm; then breathing subtlest damps,
Mix'd their own venom with the rain from Heaven,
That I woke poison'd! But, all praise to Him
Who gives us all things, more have yielded me
Permanent shelter; and beside one Friend,

Beneath the impervious covert of one oak,
I've rais'd a lowly shed, and know the names
Of Husband and of Father; not unhearing
Of that divine and nightly-whispering Voice,
Which from my childhood to maturer years
Spake to me of predestinated wreaths,
Bright with no fading colours!

                            Yet at times
My soul is sad, that I have roam'd through life
Still most a stranger, most with naked heart
At mine own home and birth-place: chiefly then,
When I remember thee, my earliest Friend!
Thee, who didst watch my boyhood and my youth;
Didst trace my wanderings with a father's eye;
And boding evil yet still hoping good,
Rebuk'd each fault, and over all my woes
Sorrow'd in silence! He who counts alone
The beatings of the solitary heart,
That Being knows, how I have lov'd thee ever,
Lov'd as a brother, as a son rever'd thee!
Oh! 'tis to me an ever new delight,
To talk of thee and thine: or when the blast
Of the shrill winter, rattling our rude sash,
Endears the cleanly hearth and social bowl;
Or when, as now, on some delicious eve,
We in our sweet sequester'd orchard-plot
Sit on the tree crook'd earth-ward; whose old boughs,
That hang above us in an arborous roof,
Stirr'd by the faint gale of departing May,
Send their loose blossoms slanting o'er our heads!

    Nor dost not thou sometimes recall those hours,
When with the joy of hope thou gavest thine ear
To my wild firstling-lays. Since then my song

Hath sounded deeper notes, such as beseem
Or that sad wisdom folly leaves behind,
Or such as, tuned to these tumultuous times,
Cope with the tempest's swell!

These various strains,
Which I have fram'd in many a various mood,
Accept, my Brother! and (for some perchance
Will strike discordant on thy milder mind)
If aught of error or intemperate truth
Should meet thine ear, think thou that riper Age
Will calm it down, and let thy love forgive it!

It was originally intended as a dedication to the 1797 collection of poems, but old brother George was 'displeased and thought his character endangered by the Dedication'.

In early June, the first draft of *Osorio* completed, Coleridge visited Wordsworth, walking (via some preaching work at the Unitarian chapel in Bridgwater) to Racedown in Dorset where William was living with his sister Dorothy in a house lent to them by John Pinney (the wealthy merchant in whose Bristol home Coleridge and Wordsworth had first met). Coleridge and Dorothy warmed to each other at once; she described her first impressions:

He is a wonderful man. His conversation teems with soul, mind and spirit. Then he is so benevolent, so good tempered and cheerful, and, like William, interests himself so much about every little trifle.

At first I thought him very plain, that is, for about three minutes; he is pale and thin, has a wide mouth, thick lips, and not very good teeth, longish loose-growing half-curling rough black hair. But if you hear him speak for five minutes you think no more of them.

His eye is large and full, not dark but grey; such an eye as would receive from a heavy soul the dullest expression; but it speaks every emotion of his animated mind; it has more of the 'poet's eye in a fine frenzy rolling' than I ever witnessed...

Coleridge would write that he, William and Dorothy were 'three persons and one soul'.

After a spell at Racedown together, in which the two poets read their work to one another (Coleridge had brought a draft of his tragedy along on his visit), Coleridge returned to his wife and child at Stowey – bringing Wordsworth with him. In early July they were back to Dorset to collect Dorothy, and the Wordsworths decided to stay in Somerset. They loved the setting, but the main draw was their friend – 'Our principal inducement,' wrote Dorothy, 'was Coleridge's company.' So the Wordsworths took Alfoxden Park, a large country-house a couple of miles from the Coleridges' on the edge of the Quantocks, another arrangement for which they had Thomas Poole to thank. 'Wherever we turn we have woods,' wrote Dorothy, 'smooth downs, and valleys with small brooks running down through green meadows...'

So, now the Wordsworths had moved in nearby; and Coleridge had other visitors this summer, too.

There was 'Citizen' John Thelwall, the revolutionary poet (who by this point had already spent some time in the Tower), who contemplated staying for good but was dissuaded. Of this visitor Coleridge remembered:

John Thelwall had something very good about him. We were once sitting in a beautiful recess in the Quantocks, when I said to him, 'Citizen John, this is a fine place to talk treason in!' – 'Nay! Citizen Samuel,' replied he, 'it is rather a place to make a man forget that there is any necessity for treason!'

And there was Coleridge's old school-friend Charles Lamb, who arrived this summer for a restorative visit (his sister Mary having in an attack of madness the previous autumn murdered their mother). Coleridge and Wordsworth were both profound lovers of natural landscape – and this local natural landscape in particular – and were enthusiastic walkers too, so on 4th July a walk with the visiting Lamb (who did not like the countryside one bit…) was planned. But there was an accident – Sara spilled boiling milk over Coleridge's foot, leaving him unable to walk. So his friends went to walk without him, and he remained, trapped in Poole's garden, contemplating his situation, imagining his friends' walk, and writing an extremely lovely poem.

This Lime-Tree Bower My Prison
[Adressed to Charles Lamb,
of the India House, London]

Well, they are gone, and here must I remain,
This lime-tree bower my prison! I have lost
Beauties and feelings, such as would have been
Most sweet to my remembrance even when age
Had dimm'd mine eyes to blindness! They, meanwhile,
Friends, whom I never more may meet again,
On springy heath, along the hill-top edge,
Wander in gladness, and wind down, perchance,
To that still roaring dell, of which I told;
The roaring dell, o'erwooded, narrow, deep,
And only speckled by the mid-day sun;
Where its slim trunk the ash from rock to rock
Flings arching like a bridge; – that branchless ash,
Unsunn'd and damp, whose few poor yellow leaves
Ne'er tremble in the gale, yet tremble still,
Fann'd by the water-fall! and there my friends
Behold the dark green file of long lank weeds,

That all at once (a most fantastic sight!)
Still nod and drip beneath the dripping edge
Of the blue clay-stone.

                    Now, my friends emerge
Beneath the wide wide Heaven—and view again
The many-steepled tract magnificent
Of hilly fields and meadows, and the sea,
With some fair bark, perhaps, whose sails light up
The slip of smooth clear blue betwixt two Isles
Of purple shadow! Yes! they wander on
In gladness all; but thou, methinks, most glad,
My gentle-hearted Charles! for thou hast pined
And hunger'd after Nature, many a year,
In the great City pent, winning thy way
With sad yet patient soul, through evil and pain
And strange calamity! Ah! slowly sink
Behind the western ridge, thou glorious Sun!
Shine in the slant beams of the sinking orb,
Ye purple heath-flowers! richlier burn, ye clouds!
Live in the yellow light, ye distant groves!
And kindle, thou blue Ocean! So my friend
Struck with deep joy may stand, as I have stood,
Silent with swimming sense; yea, gazing round
On the wide landscape, gaze till all doth seem
Less gross than bodily; and of such hues
As veil the Almighty Spirit, when yet he makes
Spirits perceive his presence.

                              A delight
Comes sudden on my heart, and I am glad
As I myself were there! Nor in this bower,
This little lime-tree bower, have I not mark'd
Much that has sooth'd me. Pale beneath the blaze
Hung the transparent foliage; and I watch'd

Some broad and sunny leaf, and lov'd to see
The shadow of the leaf and stem above
Dappling its sunshine! And that walnut-tree
Was richly ting'd, and a deep radiance lay
Full on the ancient ivy, which usurps
Those fronting elms, and now, with blackest mass
Makes their dark branches gleam a lighter hue
Through the late twilight: and though now the bat
Wheels silent by, and not a swallow twitters,
Yet still the solitary humble-bee
Sings in the bean-flower! Henceforth I shall know
That Nature ne'er deserts the wise and pure;
No plot so narrow, be but Nature there,
No waste so vacant, but may well employ
Each faculty of sense, and keep the heart
Awake to Love and Beauty! and sometimes
'Tis well to be bereft of promis'd good,
That we may lift the soul, and contemplate
With lively joy the joys we cannot share.
My gentle-hearted Charles! when the last rook
Beat its straight path across the dusky air
Homewards, I blest it! deeming its black wing
(Now a dim speck, now vanishing in light)
Had cross'd the mighty Orb's dilated glory,
While thou stood'st gazing; or, when all was still,
Flew creeking o'er thy head, and had a charm
For thee, my gentle-hearted Charles, to whom
No sound is dissonant which tells of Life.

As holy and enchanted...

Coleridge and the Wordsworths spent most of the next year together, exploring the landscape around Nether Stowey and Alfoxden Park; they talked and talked, they read their work to each other. There would be long walks – Lynmouth and Linton, along the Somerset coast – on which, Dorothy recalled, the poets made great plans.

A suspicion soon got around about the odd goings-on at Alfoxden Park (late-night walks, scribbling things in notebooks, etc.), and the suggestion was mooted somewhere by someone that the residents were perhaps foreign spies. The relationship between France and England being what it was, tensions were particularly high this year, and those Cumberland-born Wordsworths didn't have acceptable local accents, and so were almost certainly dangerous radical lunatic foreign types. So a government agent was despatched to the area – he stayed at the Globe Inn near Poole's – to investigate. After some intelligence work (where, Coleridge recalled, 'he often heard me talk of one *Spy Nozy*'), he concluded that the people under surveillance were 'violent democrats', but at least they were English. And though odd, probably harmless.

Early in October (most probably – the dates, perhaps appropriately for this particular story, are hazy and subject to much question), Coleridge walked a familiar path from Porlock to Linton, and being taken ill on his return journey stopped off in a little farmhouse (probably Ash Farm, above Culbone Church), where he took "two grains" of opium, and fell asleep in the middle of reading a line from *Purchas's Pilgrimage*. What followed – or at least Coleridge's version of what followed – has become one of the most famous of all anecdotes of a creative moment. During his sleep, Coleridge tells us in his Preface:

> … he has the most vivid confidence, that he could not have composed less than from two to three hundred lines; if that indeed can be called composition in which all the images rose up before him as *things*, with a parallel production of the correspondent expressions, without any sensation or consciousness of effort. On awaking he appeared to him-self to have a distinct recollection of the whole, and taking his pen, ink, and paper, instantly and eagerly wrote the lines that are here preserved. At this moment he was unfortun-ately called out by a person on business from Porlock, and detained by him above an hour, and on his return to his room, found, to his no small surprise and mortification, that though he still retained some vague and dim recol-lection of the general purport of the vision, yet, with the exception of some eight or ten scattered lines and images, all the rest had passed away like images on the surface of a stream into which a stone has been cast, but, alas!, with-out the after restoration of the latter!

Now, whether or not the poem was dreamed, whether there was ever more than the fifty-four lines of it we have, whether a person on business from Porlock did knock on the door and bend the poet's ear for so long that every last trace of the unwritten poem dissipated – we won't know, we can't know. Complete or incomplete, we have what we have, which is a fifty-four-line poetic vision – sustained, intense and musical, a sequence of vivid dream-images, each one crystallising and growing into the next, which may mean something symbolically, or may be just the visual sequence it immediately appears to be. Either way, this 'psychological curiosity', as Coleridge would call it, is astonishing.

Kubla Khan

In Xanadu did Kubla Khan
A stately pleasure-dome decree:
Where Alph, the sacred river, ran
Through caverns measureless to man
    Down to a sunless sea.
So twice five miles of fertile ground
With walls and towers were girdled round:
And there were gardens bright with sinuous rills,
Where blossomed many an incense-bearing tree;
And here were forests ancient as the hills,
Enfolding sunny spots of greenery.

But oh! that deep romantic chasm which slanted
Down the green hill athwart a cedarn cover!
A savage place! as holy and enchanted
As e'er beneath a waning moon was haunted
By woman wailing for her demon-lover!
And from this chasm, with ceaseless turmoil seething,
As if this earth in fast thick pants were breathing,
A mighty fountain momently was forced:
Amid whose swift half-intermitted burst
Huge fragments vaulted like rebounding hail,
Or chaffy grain beneath the thresher's flail:
And 'mid these dancing rocks at once and ever
It flung up momently the sacred river.
Five miles meandering with a mazy motion
Through wood and dale the sacred river ran,
Then reached the caverns measureless to man,

And sank in tumult to a lifeless ocean:
And 'mid this tumult Kubla heard from far
Ancestral voices prophesying war!
    The shadow of the dome of pleasure
    Floated midway on the waves;
    Where was heard the mingled measure
    From the fountain and the caves.
It was a miracle of rare device,
A sunny pleasure-dome with caves of ice!

    A damsel with a dulcimer
    In a vision once I saw:
    It was an Abyssinian maid,
    And on her dulcimer she played,
    Singing of Mount Abora.
    Could I revive within me
    Her symphony and song,
    To such a deep delight 'twould win me,
That with music loud and long,
I would build that dome in air,
That sunny dome! those caves of ice!
And all who heard should see them there,
And all should cry, Beware! Beware!
His flashing eyes, his floating hair!
Weave a circle round him thrice,
And close your eyes with holy dread,
For he on honey-dew hath fed,
And drunk the milk of Paradise.

For something that's meant to be only a 'fragment' of a poem, that's quite an ending.

Another long walk, on 13th November, gave Coleridge the seed for the poem with which he would always be most closely associated. Walking with the Wordsworths, the idea was suggested for a ballad – to be produced by the two poets in collaboration – on a supernatural theme. Though planned for a joint piece of work, it was gradually appropriated by Coleridge, who was writing the supernatural pieces (as opposed to Wordsworth's poems of rural life); Coleridge had already created 'Kubla Khan', after all, and would soon be setting out on the first part of his mysterious Gothic-influenced fairytale-like ballad, 'Christabel'. He would write, 'In poetry, whether metrical or unbound, the super-natural will be impressive and will obtain a mastery over the Imagination and feelings, will tend to infect the reader'; in turn 'The Poet must always be in perfect sympathy with the Subject of the Narrative, and tell his tale with "a most believing mind".'

This new ballad took up much of Coleridge's winter energies. It would tell a guilt-and-redemption story of a sailor on a long sea-journey who – for reasons never explained – shoots and kills an albatross that has been flying with the ship, an albatross that has brought the ship good luck and a fair wind. As a reminder of his crime, the albatross is hung round the Mariner's neck.

The Mariner's story then descends into a ghastly nightmare. A ghost ship appears, in which Death and Life-in-Death are playing at dice – the Mariner himself is the stake they play for, and Life-in-Death wins him, and Death his shipmates.

> Her *lips were red,* her *looks were free,*
> *Her locks were yellow as gold:*
> *Her skin was as white as leprosy,*
> *The Night-mare LIFE-IN-DEATH was she,*
> *Who thicks man's blood with cold.*
>
> *The naked hulk alongside came,*
> *And the twain were casting dice;*
> *'The game is done! I've won! I've won!'*
> *Quoth she, and whistles thrice.*

The Sun's rim dips; the stars rush out:
At one stride comes the dark;
With far-heard whisper, o'er the sea,
Off shot the spectre-bark.

We listened and looked sideways up!
Fear at my heart, as at a cup,
My life-blood seemed to sip!
The stars were dim, and thick the night,
The steersman's face by his lamp gleamed white;
From the sails the dew did drip –
Till clomb above the eastern bar
The hornéd Moon, with one bright star
Within the nether tip.

One after one, by the star-dogged Moon,
Too quick for groan or sigh,
Each turned his face with a ghastly pang,
And cursed me with his eye.

Four times fifty living men,
(And I heard nor sigh nor groan)
With heavy thump, a lifeless lump,
They dropped down one by one.

The crew are all dead – all but the Mariner, who is left

Alone, alone, all, all alone,
Alone on a wide wide sea!
And never a saint took pity on
My soul in agony.

He is tortured with thirst (that much misquoted 'Water, water everywhere…') but is unable to die. And then, suddenly, the mariner finds in himself the capacity to see the beauty in the sea-snakes beside the ship:

> *Beyond the shadow of the ship,*
> *I watched the water-snakes:*
> *They moved in tracks of shining white*
> *And when they reared, the elfish light*
> *Fell off in hoary flakes.*

> *Within the shadow of the ship*
> *I watched their rich attire:*
> *Blue, glossy green, and velvet black,*
> *They coiled and swam; and every track*
> *Was a flash of golden fire.*

And this moment of his recognising and blessing the beauty of God's creatures redeems him – the albatross falls from his neck, and he can sleep. He awakes to rain – and quenches his thirst – and sees the crew rise up (still dead) and work the ropes to get the ship moving, and the mariner is rescued. But his penance is not quite done – he is obliged to go from place to place, forever, finding people to whom he must repeat his tale, and its moral:

> *He prayeth well, who loveth well*
> *Both man and bird and beast.*

> *He prayeth best, who loveth best*
> *All things both great and small;*
> *For the dear God who loveth us,*
> *He made and loveth all.*

Part of the story came from the dream of a friend, John Cruickshank, about a curse and a skeleton-ship; other parts, including the murder of the albatross, were ideas of Wordsworth's.

On 23rd March, Coleridge walked to Alfoxden carrying the finished manuscript of 'The Rime of the Ancient Mariner' to read to his friend.

> It is an ancient Mariner,
> And he stoppeth one of three.
> 'By thy long grey beard and glittering eye,
> Now wherefore stopp'st thou me?
>
> The Bridegroom's doors are opened wide,
> And I am next of kin;
> The guests are met, the feast is set:
> May'st hear the merry din.'
>
> He holds him with his skinny hand,
> 'There was a ship,' quoth he.
> 'Hold off! unhand me, grey-beard loon!'
> Eftsoons his hand dropt he.
>
> He holds him with his glittering eye –
> The Wedding-Guest stood still,
> And listens like a three years' child:
> The Mariner hath his will.
>
> The Wedding-Guest sat on a stone:
> He cannot choose but hear;
> And thus spake on that ancient man,
> The bright-eyed Mariner.
>
> 'The ship was cheered, the harbour cleared,
> Merrily did we drop
> Below the kirk, below the hill,
> Below the lighthouse top.

The Sun came up upon the left,
Out of the sea came he!
And he shone bright, and on the right
Went down into the sea.

[…]

'And now the STORM-BLAST came, and he
Was tyrannous and strong:
He struck with his o'ertaking wings,
And chased us south along.

With sloping masts and dipping prow,
As who pursued with yell and blow
Still treads the shadow of his foe,
And forward bends his head,
The ship drove fast, loud roared the blast,
And southward aye we fled.

And now there came both mist and snow,
And it grew wondrous cold:
And ice, mast-high, came floating by,
As green as emerald…

Over the winter of 1797–8 Coleridge would be hard at work on the 'Mariner', but he was dividing his time between this great project and a number of other significant pieces too.

In February 1798 he would write two major works, quite different from each other in every respect – subject, style, tone. The first was a meditation on his sleeping child, and on his own childhood – the church bells of Ottery, schooldays at Christ's Hospital. Coleridge would be (on balance) happy throughout this most productive period in his poetic life – happy even in his marriage; and his optimism and contentment are palpable in 'Frost at Midnight':

Frost at Midnight

The Frost performs its secret ministry,
Unhelped by any wind. The owlet's cry
Came loud – and hark, again! loud as before.
The inmates of my cottage, all at rest,
Have left me to that solitude, which suits
Abstruser musings: save that at my side
My cradled infant slumbers peacefully.
'Tis calm indeed! so calm, that it disturbs
And vexes meditation with its strange
And extreme silentness. Sea, hill, and wood,
This populous village! Sea, and hill, and wood,
With all the numberless goings-on of life,
Inaudible as dreams! the thin blue flame
Lies on my low-burnt fire, and quivers not;
Only that film, which fluttered on the grate,
Still flutters there, the sole unquiet thing.
Methinks, its motion in this hush of nature
Gives it dim sympathies with me who live,
Making it a companionable form,
Whose puny flaps and freaks the idling Spirit
By its own moods interprets, every where
Echo or mirror seeking of itself,
And makes a toy of Thought.

But O! how oft,
How oft, at school, with most believing mind,
Presageful, have I gazed upon the bars,
To watch that fluttering stranger! and as oft
With unclosed lids, already had I dreamt
Of my sweet birth-place, and the old church-tower,
Whose bells, the poor man's only music, rang
From morn to evening, all the hot Fair-day,
So sweetly, that they stirred and haunted me

With a wild pleasure, falling on mine ear
Most like articulate sounds of things to come!
So gazed I, till the soothing things, I dreamt,
Lulled me to sleep, and sleep prolonged my dreams!
And so I brooded all the following morn,
Awed by the stern preceptor's face, mine eye
Fixed with mock study on my swimming book:
Save if the door half opened, and I snatched
A hasty glance, and still my heart leaped up,
For still I hoped to see the stranger's face,
Townsman, or aunt, or sister more beloved,
My play-mate when we both were clothed alike!

Dear Babe, that sleepest cradled by my side,
Whose gentle breathings, heard in this deep calm,
Fill up the intersperséd vacancies
And momentary pauses of the thought!
My babe so beautiful! it thrills my heart
With tender gladness, thus to look at thee,
And think that thou shalt learn far other lore,
And in far other scenes! For I was reared
In the great city, pent 'mid cloisters dim,
And saw nought lovely but the sky and stars.
But thou, my babe! shalt wander like a breeze
By lakes and sandy shores, beneath the crags
Of ancient mountain, and beneath the clouds,
Which image in their bulk both lakes and shores
And mountain crags: so shalt thou see and hear
The lovely shapes and sounds intelligible
Of that eternal language, which thy God
Utters, who from eternity doth teach
Himself in all, and all things in himself.
Great universal Teacher! he shall mould
Thy spirit, and by giving make it ask.

Therefore all seasons shall be sweet to thee,
Whether the summer clothe the general earth
With greenness, or the redbreast sit and sing
Betwixt the tufts of snow on the bare branch
Of mossy apple-tree, while the nigh thatch
Smokes in the sun-thaw; whether the eave-drops fall
Heard only in the trances of the blast,
Or if the secret ministry of frost
Shall hang them up in silent icicles,
Quietly shining to the quiet Moon.

'Frost' was followed by 'France: An Ode', in which we read Coleridge's terrible disenchantment at post-revolutionary France, and in particular the invasion of neutral Switzerland:

France: An Ode

I

Ye Clouds! that far above me float and pause,
Whose pathless march no mortal may controul!
Ye Ocean-Waves! that, wheresoe'er ye roll,
Yield homage only to eternal laws!
Ye Woods! that listen to the night-birds singing,
Midway the smooth and perilous slope reclined,
Save when your own imperious branches swinging,
Have made a solemn music of the wind!
Where, like a man beloved of God,
Through glooms, which never woodman trod,
How oft, pursuing fancies holy,
My moonlight way o'er flowering weeds I wound,
Inspired, beyond the guess of folly,
By each rude shape and wild unconquerable sound!

O ye loud Waves! and O ye Forests high!
  And O ye Clouds that far above me soared!
Thou rising Sun! thou blue rejoicing Sky!
  Yea, every thing that is and will be free!
Bear witness for me, wheresoe'er ye be,
  With what deep worship I have still adored
    The spirit of divinest Liberty.

II

When France in wrath her giant-limbs upreared,
  And with that oath, which smote air, earth, and sea,
  Stamped her strong foot and said she would be free,
Bear witness for me, how I hoped and feared!
With what a joy my lofty gratulation
  Unawed I sang, amid a slavish band:
And when to whelm the disenchanted nation,
  Like fiends embattled by a wizard's wand,
    The Monarchs marched in evil day,
    And Britain join'd the dire array;
  Though dear her shores and circling ocean,
Though many friendships, many youthful loves
  Had swol'n the patriot emotion
And flung a magic light o'er all her hills and groves;
Yet still my voice, unaltered, sang defeat
  To all that braved the tyrant-quelling lance,
And shame too long delay'd and vain retreat!
For ne'er, O Liberty! with partial aim
I dimmed thy light or damped thy holy flame;
  But blessed the paeans of delivered France,
And hung my head and wept at Britain's name.

III

'And what,' I said, 'though Blasphemy's loud scream
  With that sweet music of deliverance strove!

Though all the fierce and drunken passions wove
A dance more wild than e'er was maniac's dream!
  Ye storms, that round the dawning east assembled,
The Sun was rising, though ye hid his light!'
  And when, to soothe my soul, that hoped and trembled,
The dissonance ceased, and all seemed calm and bright;
    When France her front deep-scarr'd and gory
    Concealed with clustering wreaths of glory;
      When, insupportably advancing,
    Her arm made mockery of the warrior's ramp;
      While timid looks of fury glancing,
    Domestic treason, crushed beneath her fatal stamp,
Writhed like a wounded dragon in his gore;
  Then I reproached my fears that would not flee;
'And soon,' I said, 'shall Wisdom teach her lore
In the low huts of them that toil and groan!
And, conquering by her happiness alone,
    Shall France compel the nations to be free,
Till Love and Joy look round, and call the Earth their own.'

IV

Forgive me, Freedom! O forgive those dreams!
  I hear thy voice, I hear thy loud lament,
  From bleak Helvetia's icy caverns sent –
I hear thy groans upon her blood-stained streams!
  Heroes, that for your peaceful country perished,
And ye that, fleeing, spot your mountain-snows
  With bleeding wounds; forgive me, that I cherished
One thought that ever blessed your cruel foes!
    To scatter rage and traitorous guilt,
    Where Peace her jealous home had built;
      A patriot-race to disinherit
Of all that made their stormy wilds so dear;
      And with inexpiable spirit

To taint the bloodless freedom of the mountaineer –
O France, that mockest Heaven, adulterous, blind,
    And patriot only in pernicious toils!
Are these thy boasts, Champion of human kind?
    To mix with Kings in the low lust of sway,
Yell in the hunt, and share the murderous prey;
To insult the shrine of Liberty with spoils
    From freemen torn; to tempt and to betray?

v

    The Sensual and the Dark rebel in vain,
    Slaves by their own compulsion! In mad game
    They burst their manacles and wear the name
        Of Freedom, graven on a heavier chain!
    O Liberty! with profitless endeavour
Have I pursued thee, many a weary hour;
    But thou nor swell'st the victor's strain, nor ever
Didst breathe thy soul in forms of human power.
    Alike from all, howe'er they praise thee,
    (Nor prayer, nor boastful name delays thee)
        Alike from Priestcraft's harpy minions,
    And factious Blasphemy's obscener slaves,
        Thou speedest on thy subtle pinions,
The guide of homeless winds, and playmate of the waves!
And there I felt thee! – on that sea-cliff's verge,
    Whose pines, scarce travelled by the breeze above,
    Had made one murmur with the distant surge!
Yes, while I stood and gazed, my temples bare,
And shot my being through earth, sea and air,
    Possessing all things with intensest love,
O Liberty! my spirit felt thee there.

The state of the political world and its impact on English life prompted Coleridge's next major piece, 'Fears in Solitude', written in April; the subtitle of this poem is 'Written in April 1798, during the alarm of an invasion'. A reluctantly trimmed-down version follows:

from **Fears in Solitude**

A green and silent spot, amid the hills,
A small and silent dell! O'er stiller place
No singing sky-lark ever poised himself.
The hills are heathy, save that swelling slope,
Which hath a gay and gorgeous covering on,
All golden with the never-bloomless furze,
Which now blooms most profusely: but the dell,
Bathed by the mist, is fresh and delicate
As vernal corn-field, or the unripe flax,
When, through its half-transparent stalks, at eve,
The level sunshine glimmers with green light.
Oh! 'tis a quiet spirit-healing nook!
Which all, methinks, would love; but chiefly he,
The humble man, who, in his youthful years,
Knew just so much of folly, as had made
His early manhood more securely wise!
Here he might lie on fern or withered heath,
While from the singing lark (that sings unseen
The minstrelsy that solitude loves best),
And from the sun, and from the breezy air,
Sweet influences trembled o'er his frame;
And he, with many feelings, many thoughts,
Made up a meditative joy, and found
Religious meanings in the forms of Nature!
And so, his senses gradually wrapt
In a half sleep, he dreams of better worlds,
And dreaming hears thee still, O singing lark,
That singest like an angel in the clouds!

My God! it is a melancholy thing
For such a man, who would full fain preserve
His soul in calmness, yet perforce must feel
For all his human brethren – O my God!
It weighs upon the heart, that he must think
What uproar and what strife may now be stirring
This way or that way o'er these silent hills –
Invasion, and the thunder and the shout,
And all the crash of onset; fear and rage,
And undetermined conflict – even now,
Even now, perchance, and in his native isle:
Carnage and groans beneath this blessed sun!
We have offended, Oh! my countrymen!
We have offended very grievously,
And been most tyrannous. From east to west
A groan of accusation pierces Heaven!
The wretched plead against us; multitudes
Countless and vehement, the sons of God,
Our brethren! Like a cloud that travels on,
Steamed up from Cairo's swamps of pestilence,
Even so, my countrymen! have we gone forth
And borne to distant tribes slavery and pangs,
And, deadlier far, our vices, whose deep taint
With slow perdition murders the whole man,
His body and his soul! Meanwhile, at home,
All individual dignity and power
Engulfed in Courts, Committees, Institutions,
Associations and Societies,
A vain, speech-mouthing, speech-reporting Guild,
One Benefit-Club for mutual flattery,
We have drunk up, demure as at a grace,
Pollutions from the brimming cup of wealth;
Contemptuous of all honourable rule,
Yet bartering freedom and the poor man's life
For gold, as at a market! The sweet words

Of Christian promise, words that even yet
Might stem destruction, were they wisely preached,
Are muttered o'er by men, whose tones proclaim
How flat and wearisome they feel their trade:
Rank scoffers some, but most too indolent
To deem them falsehoods or to know their truth.
Oh! blasphemous! the Book of Life is made
A superstitious instrument, on which
We gabble o'er the oaths we mean to break;
For all must swear – all and in every place,
College and wharf, council and justice-court;
All, all must swear, the briber and the bribed,
Merchant and lawyer, senator and priest,
The rich, the poor, the old man and the young;
All, all make up one scheme of perjury,
That faith doth reel; the very name of God
Sounds like a juggler's charm; and, bold with joy,
Forth from his dark and lonely hiding-place,
(Portentous sight!) the owlet Atheism,
Sailing on obscene wings athwart the noon,
Drops his blue-fringéd lids, and holds them close,
And hooting at the glorious sun in Heaven,
Cries out, 'Where is it?'

[...]

But now the gentle dew-fall sends abroad
The fruit-like perfume of the golden furze:
The light has left the summit of the hill,
Though still a sunny gleam lies beautiful,
Aslant the ivied beacon. Now farewell,
Farewell, awhile, O soft and silent spot!
On the green sheep-track, up the heathy hill,
Homeward I wind my way; and lo! recalled
From bodings that have well-nigh wearied me,

I find myself upon the brow, and pause
Startled! And after lonely sojourning
In such a quiet and surrounded nook,
This burst of prospect, here the shadowy main,
Dim tinted, there the mighty majesty
Of that huge amphitheatre of rich
And elmy fields, seems like society –
Conversing with the mind, and giving it
A livelier impulse and a dance of thought!
And now, belovéd Stowey! I behold
Thy church-tower, and, methinks, the four huge elms
Clustering, which mark the mansion of my friend;
And close behind them, hidden from my view,
Is my own lowly cottage, where my babe
And my babe's mother dwell in peace! With light
And quickened footsteps thitherward I tend,
Remembering thee, O green and silent dell!
And grateful, that by nature's quietness
And solitary musings, all my heart
Is softened, and made worthy to indulge
Love, and the thoughts that yearn for human kind.

'Fears in Solitude', 'Frost at Midnight' and 'France: An Ode' (which *The Morning Post* published first in April) appeared together in a smart little quarto pamphlet in the autumn of this year.

Amid all the poetry-writing frenzy of the opening months of 1798, Coleridge also found time to carry out a large amount of other work, preaching at the Mary Street Unitarian Chapel in Taunton (standing in for the lately bereaved Revd Joshua Toulmin) and at Shrewsbury. It was at this latter engagement in January that he was heard by the young essayist William Hazlitt, who would describe the performance in *On My First Acquaintance with Poets*:

… Mr Coleridge rose and gave out his text, 'And he went up into the mountains to pray, HIMSELF, ALONE.' As he gave out this text, his voice 'rose like a steam of rich distilled perfumes'; and when he came to the last two words, which he pronounced loud, deep, and distinct, it seemed to me, who was then young, as if the sounds had echoed from the bottom of the human heart, and as if that prayer might have floated in solemn silence through the universe…

Coleridge's promising career as a Unitarian preacher would soon come to an abrupt stop. The reasons were two-fold, one practical and one spiritual. The first was simple, as an annuity from a pair of generous friends granted to him now made it less necessary that he dash about trying to claw together a living and could instead stay home and write; and the second was the realisation that his once-steadfast faith was beginning to be undercut by slight uncertainties – for much of the rest of his life his faith would be the object of occasional challenges, though he would always find a way back in.

The annuity, from the Wedgwood brothers, Thomas and Josiah, would allow Coleridge a significant £150, enabling him to devote himself to his poetry and his philosophy.

And so he did – with Wordsworth the loyal midwife to this work.

Out of the poets' endless discussions an idea was forming now – a big idea. The creation of a collection of poems that would be unlike anything anyone had seen before – it would be (so Wordsworth and Coleridge planned) a new kind of poetry, poetry using a new kind of language, on the sorts of subjects usually ignored by poets. It would be a language of every day – quite different to the deliberately hyper-poetic language used in poetry through most of the eighteenth century – which would make the poems accessible; and they would deal with the lives of rural people, simple people, not confine themselves to the grand, or the upper-class-bound, or the epic. The collection would be an experiment, introducing a radical, new poetry – and it would be called the *Lyrical Ballads*. It would be a gesture, as bold as they come.

Among all these poems of everyday life told in everyday language, the plan was to include 'The Ancient Mariner'. But of course it is a supernatural tale, albeit told with clarity of vision as though describing reality, with real physicality of sensations. As a supernatural tale – and one often with old-style phrases, with those amazingly strong unearthly visual images – it is not exactly a typical plain-language tale of rural life, an extremely odd fit for the planned new collection. There is really nothing in the *Lyrical Ballads* like it. Arguably, of course, there is nothing like it anywhere else either.

The rural life was being well served by another pen, however. Wordsworth was going through his own rich period of creativity this year, especially this spring, producing work that demonstrated his own sense of wonder at the world around him, and which would represent his contribution to the *Lyrical Ballads* – enduring poems like 'We Are Seven', 'The Idiot Boy', 'The Old Cumberland Beggar', 'Simon Lee' and 'Lines Written a Few Miles above Tintern Abbey'. And as part of his contribution Coleridge came up with 'The Nightingale' after another Linton/Lynmouth coastal walk, this time with the visiting Hazlitt, on which the two men discussed birds in poetry. 'The Nightingale' he described as a 'conversation poem', a phrase he would use to refer to those certain works of his that represented responses to the experiences of the real world inhabited by himself and his friends.

The Nightingale
A Conversation Poem, April, 1798

No cloud, no relique of the sunken day
Distinguishes the West, no long thin slip

Of sullen light, no obscure trembling hues.
Come, we will rest on this old mossy bridge!
You see the glimmer of the stream beneath,
But hear no murmuring: it flows silently,
O'er its soft bed of verdure. All is still,
A balmy night! and though the stars be dim,
Yet let us think upon the vernal showers
That gladden the green earth, and we shall find
A pleasure in the dimness of the stars.
And hark! the Nightingale begins its song,
'Most musical, most melancholy' bird!
A melancholy bird? Oh! idle thought!
In Nature there is nothing melancholy.
But some night-wandering man whose heart was pierced
With the remembrance of a grievous wrong,
Or slow distemper, or neglected love,
(And so, poor wretch! filled all things with himself,
And made all gentle sounds tell back the tale
Of his own sorrow) he, and such as he,
First named these notes a melancholy strain.
And many a poet echoes the conceit;
Poet who hath been building up the rhyme
When he had better far have stretched his limbs
Beside a brook in mossy forest-dell,
By sun or moon-light, to the influxes
Of shapes and sounds and shifting elements
Surrendering his whole spirit, of his song
And of his fame forgetful! so his fame
Should share in Nature's immortality,
A venerable thing! and so his song
Should make all Nature lovelier, and itself
Be loved like Nature! But 'twill not be so;
And youths and maidens most poetical,
Who lose the deepening twilights of the spring
In ball-rooms and hot theatres, they still

Full of meek sympathy must heave their sighs
O'er Philomela's pity-pleading strains.

My Friend, and thou, our Sister! we have learnt
A different lore: we may not thus profane
Nature's sweet voices, always full of love
And joyance! 'Tis the merry Nightingale
That crowds, and hurries, and precipitates
With fast thick warble his delicious notes,
As he were fearful that an April night
Would be too short for him to utter forth
His love-chant, and disburthen his full soul
Of all its music!
                                    And I know a grove
Of large extent, hard by a castle huge,
Which the great lord inhabits not; and so
This grove is wild with tangling underwood,
And the trim walks are broken up, and grass,
Thin grass and king-cups grow within the paths.
But never elsewhere in one place I knew
So many nightingales; and far and near,
In wood and thicket, over the wide grove,
They answer and provoke each other's song,
With skirmish and capricious passagings,
And murmurs musical and swift jug jug,
And one low piping sound more sweet than all –
Stirring the air with such a harmony,
That should you close your eyes, you might almost
Forget it was not day! On moonlight bushes,
Whose dewy leaflets are but half-disclosed,
You may perchance behold them on the twigs,
Their bright, bright eyes, their eyes both bright and full,
Glistening, while many a glow-worm in the shade
Lights up her love-torch.

A most gentle Maid,
Who dwelleth in her hospitable home
Hard by the castle, and at latest eve
(Even like a Lady vowed and dedicate
To something more than Nature in the grove)
Glides through the pathways; she knows all their notes,
That gentle Maid! and oft, a moment's space,
What time the moon was lost behind a cloud,
Hath heard a pause of silence; till the moon
Emerging, hath awakened earth and sky
With one sensation, and those wakeful birds
Have all burst forth in choral minstrelsy,
As if some sudden gale had swept at once
A hundred airy harps! And she hath watched
Many a nightingale perch giddily
On blossomy twig still swinging from the breeze,
And to that motion tune his wanton song
Like tipsy Joy that reels with tossing head.

Farewell! O Warbler! till to-morrow eve,
And you, my friends! farewell, a short farewell!
We have been loitering long and pleasantly,
And now for our dear homes. – That strain again!
Full fain it would delay me! My dear babe,
Who, capable of no articulate sound,
Mars all things with his imitative lisp,
How he would place his hand beside his ear,
His little hand, the small forefinger up,
And bid us listen! And I deem it wise
To make him Nature's play-mate. He knows well
The evening-star; and once, when he awoke
In most distressful mood (some inward pain
Had made up that strange thing, an infant's dream –)
I hurried with him to our orchard-plot,
And he beheld the moon, and, hushed at once,

Suspends his sobs, and laughs most silently,
While his fair eyes, that swam with undropped tears,
Did glitter in the yellow moon-beam! Well! –
It is a father's tale: But if that Heaven
Should give me life, his childhood shall grow up
Familiar with these songs, that with the night
He may associate joy. – Once more, farewell,
Sweet Nightingale! once more, my friends! farewell.

The poem was sent to Alfoxden with a note:

In stale blank verse a subject stale
I send per post my Nightingale
And like an honest bard, dear Wordsworth,
You'll tell me what you think, my Bird's worth...

Seven weeks after the Mariner was completed, on 14th May, a second son, Berkeley, was born to Sara Coleridge. Where Hartley's birth had come at a time of atypical domestic harmony, Berkeley arrived in a tense, unhappy – and more typical – phase in the Coleridge marriage.

By the end of the summer the great work was complete. In the event the *Lyrical Ballads* would not represent the work of its two authors evenly. Coleridge would be represented by 'The Ancient Mariner' – the longest piece in the collection and utterly anomalous in style – along with 'The Nightingale', and 'The Dungeon' and 'The Foster-mother's Tale' (both in fact originally fragments from *Osorio*); but there would be no 'Frost at Midnight', no 'Fears in Solitude', no 'Lime-Tree Bower' – the whole of the rest of the collection would be taken up by Wordsworth.

In September the collection was brought to birth by Cottle, who printed 500 copies. A brief 'Advertisement' was printed at its head explaining the poets' underpinning poetic philosophy, in particular explaining those poems which were 'written chiefly with a view to ascertain how far the language of conversation in the middle and lower classes of society is adapted to the purposes of poetic pleasure'.

But the poets would not stay to see it published. Coleridge, Wordsworth and Dorothy had been talking for some time about taking a trip together to Germany, where Coleridge could put the Wedgwood allowance towards educating himself in the European manner; two decades years later he would look back and write,

> The generous and munificent patronage of Mr Josiah and Mr Thomas Wedgwood enabled me to finish my education in Germany. Instead of troubling others with my own crude notions and juvenile compositions, I was thenceforward better employed attempting to store my own head with the wisdom of others. I made the best use of my time and means; and there is therefore no period of my life on which I can look back with such unmingled satisfaction.

Given what would happen during this excursion, to describe his satisfaction as 'unmingled' is peculiar. And his habit of filling his 'own head with the wisdom of others' would cause him plenty of trouble, too...

Wordsworth and STC set sail from Yarmouth on 16th September, leaving Sara Coleridge and the children behind them, and the presses rolling on their joint masterpiece. During their stay in Germany the *Lyrical Ballads* would be published, and with it, and with its subsequent editions, the Romantic movement in English literature would be born.

Having long been doomed to roam...

So... On 13th September, 1798, the *Lyrical Ballads* were printed in London. This collection of poems by Somerset neighbours Wordsworth and Coleridge, written in a short burst of frenzied creativity, was to herald and define a radically new spirit and sensibility for English poetry. Three days later, a packet-boat left Yarmouth for the little German harbour-town of Cuxhaven; among its passengers were the two poets, together with William's sister Dorothy and another friend, an unremarkable young farmer by the name of John Chester. This was the beginning of the merry little group's German tour, which they had planned to last around two months. Wordsworth was twenty-eight, Coleridge just twenty-six.

After a rough crossing, the party docked in Germany on 19th September. Being thrown into this strange new world quickly emphasised the differences in the natures of the two poets, and the differences in their expectations of the tour. Coleridge, the more garrulous, wanted to explore the country and the customs, to meet the people and come to know their language and their culture – to come to know them as well as his own, if possible. Wordsworth took little interest in any such things, and was instead just seeking a bit of peace and quiet, a secluded corner where he could sit and think and write undisturbed. So while the *Lyrical Ballads* were being published back home, its two authors, quite ignorant of its fate, were finding their respective places and occupations in the alien surroundings of late-eighteenth-century Saxony.

Wordsworth and Coleridge chose their German experiences quite differently. The two stories are never far apart, however; throughout their separate travels the friends remained in constant contact, each feeding off inspiration from the other – just as they used to do back in England, when they sat working in the same Somerset room night after night.

Coleridge, as he had intended, lived in Germany a life of passionate investigation – making friends, travelling alone or with Chester, taking opium, studying German and the works of the German philosophers and writers: Kant, Schelling, Schiller, Lessing, Goethe. He drank, walked, attended lectures, danced and read and read. His letters home describe with his usual wonder the strange things he encounters – from peculiar student drinking-games involving hats and swords to the quaint custom of decorating a tree for Christmas. He studied Spinozism here, too, which led to some questioning of his life-long Unitarian faith ('My head was with Spinoza, though my whole heart remained with Paul and John…'); although his faith would remain with him his whole life, Coleridge often found himself questioning it, trying to reconcile it with – for example – the pantheism he found in Spinoza, or the transcendental philosophy he read in his much-admired Kant.

Meanwhile his friend Wordsworth, whose own intensity was of a rather quieter sort, shut himself up in a room in Goslar with his sister (who continued to be a sort of Muse-cum-secretary to him) and began his own explorations, inwards; he mined his thoughts and memories and began work on his great personal epic poem, then called his 'Poem to Coleridge'. His experience was difficult; with only rudimentary German he had trouble befriending the natives – made all the more difficult since it was rarely possible even to leave his room for the bitter cold. For their German tour the poets had chosen the coldest winter in a century. The second edition of *Lyrical Ballads* would include a Wordsworth poem called simply – and rather bleakly – 'Written in Germany on one of the coldest days of the century'.

While they were apart – Coleridge travelling, talking and drinking, Wordsworth writing and contemplating and grumbling at the cold – the friends wrote frequently to one another, exchanging observations and fragments of poetry as had been their custom back in England. Each in his way had invested heavily in an experience of a peculiar intensity, and the two months stretched to three, then four, then five.

But for Coleridge it wasn't quite as simple as it may appear. It was not all wild exploration and liberating Romantic experience. For remember that this enthusiastic, frantically active, pathologically friendly Coleridge was a married man, and his wife Sara and their children were back in Somerset, eagerly awaiting his return – a return which was further postponed with every missive he sent back to them.

Coleridge wrote a little poem to his wife:

Something Childish, but Very Natural
Written in Germany

If I had but two little wings
And were a little feathery bird,
To you I'd fly, my dear!
But thoughts like these are idle things,
And I stay here.

But in my sleep to you I fly:
I'm always with you in my sleep!
The world is all one's own.
But then one wakes, and where am I?
All, all alone.

Sleep stays not, though a monarch bids:
So I love to wake ere break of day:
For though my sleep be gone,
Yet while 'tis dark, one shuts one's lids,
And still dreams on.

Innocent and sweet as this is, however, there are clear feelings of guilt and homesickness apparent in his letters of this time, but these were clearly never quite strong enough to deter him from what he sees as his greater purpose. In his absence his marriage – a relationship that had in truth been on a shaky footing since Samuel and Sara first met – began to totter yet more perilously.

In February, Coleridge's eight-month-old son Berkeley died – he had been a mere three months old when his father saw him last.

Epitaph on an Infant

Its balmy lips the infant blest
Relaxing from its Mother's breast,
How sweet it heaves the happy sigh
Of innocent satiety!

And such my Infant's latest sigh!
Oh tell, rude stone! the passer by,
That here the pretty babe doth lie,
Death sang to sleep with Lullaby.

Coleridge only heard the news a full seven weeks later, after Poole had urged Sara to keep it from him (so as not to trouble his studies); when he did at last learn Berkeley's sad fate, Coleridge was racked with guilt at having abandoned his family, and felt still more terrible pangs of homesickness. Another letter to England followed: 'My dear Poole! don't let little Hartley die before I come home. – That's silly – true – & I burst into tears as I wrote it…'

A distraught Sara entreated him to come home. Coleridge wrote back at once, trying to soothe Sara's grief and to express his own – but postponing his return, yet again.

Home-Sick
Written in Germany

'Tis sweet to him who all the week
    Through city-crowds must push his way,
To stroll alone through fields and woods,
    And hallow thus the Sabbath-day.

And sweet it is, in summer bower,
    Sincere, affectionate and gay,
One's own dear children feasting round,
    To celebrate one's marriage-day.

But what is all to his delight,
    Who having long been doomed to roam,
Throws off the bundle from his back,
    Before the door of his own home?

Home-sickness is a wasting pang;
    This feel I hourly more and more:
There's healing only in thy wings,
    Thou breeze that play'st on Albion's shore!

Meanwhile the Wordsworths had been finding the German winter rather more than they could bear. They could see no benefit in being away from home. With hindsight it is clear that it was their isolation and homesickness that partly helped to unleash the torrent of memories that Wordsworth crafted into his greatest poem; but all they could see was that they were unhappy at Goslar, Dorothy most of all, and it was *very cold*. They decided at last to return to England. Even this was not without its nuisances and delays, though; brother and sister were forced to sit out two more months of winter at Goslar, waiting till the spring thaw would open the roads and rivers and allow them to make their escape. At last in late February (by now William had also managed to complete his famous 'Lucy' poems) brother and sister left Goslar, and after some weeks' leisurely travel arrived in England on 1st May. Coleridge, they thought, could surely be left to his own devices; after all, they had hardly spent any time with him in the last four months, living their respective lives, as different as can be imagined – one manic, the other two sedentary, one garrulous, demanding, dazzling, the others reflective, self-sufficient.

Yet as winter turned to spring Coleridge did feel his friends' absence and in part blamed Dorothy. She had been keeping her brother from enjoying himself, Coleridge felt; and besides, he couldn't help some feelings of jealousy, jealousy that Dorothy and not he had been the one person Wordsworth wanted to have with him, needed to have with him, as he embarked on the work they may already have known would be his masterpiece.

Coleridge remained in Germany another three months. He studied in Ratzeburg and Göttingen, picking up ideas that would inform much of his subsequent writing. He translated and he adapted German works and assimilated their thoughts and sensibilities (this is something of a euphemism, incidentally; after his return to England he would be dogged by accusations of plagiarism…). He made many friends with whom he travelled around the country – or perhaps it would be more accurate to say that he travelled around the country and his new friends, fawning acolytes all, followed him around hanging on his every brilliant word, entranced. As was his wont he made numerous grand plans for projects about which he wrote enthusiastically to his patrons ('What have I done in Germany?' he begins, and goes on to describe his preliminary work for a life of Lessing, a history of German Belles Lettres, etc.), and completed none of them. Where once it had seemed that Wordsworth had needed Coleridge to release his poetic imagination (after all, he had moved down to Somerset expressly to be close to him), now it seemed that he had been managing quite well on his own. Coleridge, for his part, for all his excitement and stimulation in Germany, had written no poetry of note there, none at all.

And in June Coleridge finally left Göttingen for home – albeit at a leisurely pace, via a walking tour of the Brocken in the Harz mountains...

Lines: Written in the Album at Elbingerode, in the Hartz Forest

I stood on Brocken's sovran height, and saw
Woods crowding upon woods, hills over hills,
A surging scene, and only limited
By the blue distance. Heavily my way
Downward I dragged through fir groves evermore,
Where bright green moss heaves in sepulchral forms
Speckled with sunshine; and, but seldom heard,
The sweet bird's song became a hollow sound;
And the breeze, murmuring indivisibly,
Preserved its solemn murmur most distinct
From many a note of many a waterfall,
And the brook's chatter; 'mid whose islet-stones
The dingy kidling with its tinkling bell
Leaped frolicsome, or old romantic goat
Sat, his white beard slow waving. I moved on
In low and languid mood: for I had found
That outward forms, the loftiest, still receive

Their finer influence from the Life within; –
Fair cyphers else: fair, but of import vague
Or unconcerning, where the heart not finds
History or prophecy of friend, or child,
Or gentle maid, our first and early love,
Or father, or the venerable name
Of our adoréd country! O thou Queen,
Thou delegated Deity of Earth,
O dear, dear England! how my longing eye
Turned westward, shaping in the steady clouds
Thy sands and high white cliffs!

                              My native Land!
Filled with the thought of thee this heart was proud,
Yea, mine eye swam with tears: that all the view
From sovran Brocken, woods and woody hills,
Floated away, like a departing dream,
Feeble and dim! Stranger, these impulses
Blame thou not lightly; nor will I profane,
With hasty judgment or injurious doubt,
That man's sublimer spirit, who can feel
That God is everywhere! the God who framed
Mankind to be one mighty family,
Himself our Father, and the World our Home.

Genial spirits fail...

Coleridge arrived home, at last, in late July, bringing with him an entirely new German sensibility, bringing the ideas of the Enlightenment writers back to England. He was eager to get down to work, his frenzied, magpie brain buzzing, crammed with a thousand new ideas. He had been away from home for ten months.

After a very brief stay with his wife at Nether Stowey, failing to persuade Wordsworth to join him there, Coleridge set off north to see his friend instead. Part of October was spent reunited with William in Sockburn, near Darlington on the Tees in the north-east, where Wordsworth and his brother John were visiting the farm of Thomas Hutchinson. Coleridge joined the Wordsworth brothers on a walking tour of the Lake District, then returned to Sockburn, and fell desperately in love.

The object of Coleridge's passion was Sara Hutchinson, one of Thomas Hutchinson's daughters. Coleridge would nurture an impossible passion for her for the rest of his life – and write a number of poems for and about her. These are his 'Asra' poems, referring to his literary codename for Sara H, distinguishing her from the other Sara, his wife, currently in Somerset, grieving and resentful, beside their son Berkeley's tiny grave.

This new Sara – Asra – also had a sister, Mary, who in time would become Mrs William Wordsworth.

On Sunday 24th November, sitting by the fire, Coleridge held Sara's hand and 'for the first time, Love pierced me with its dart, envenomed, and alas! incurable.' He visited the now-ruined Sockburn church with her (and heard the legend of a local dragon-slaying), then sped through the composition of a ballad. Of this poem, Leigh Hunt would write, 'one of the charms of it consists in the numerous repetitions and revolvings of the words, one on the other, as if taking delight in their own beauty.'

Love

All thoughts, all passions, all delights,
Whatever stirs this mortal frame,
All are but ministers of Love,
And feed his sacred flame.

Oft in my waking dreams do I
Live o'er again that happy hour,
When midway on the mount I lay,
Beside the ruined tower.

The moonshine, stealing o'er the scene,
Had blended with the lights of eve;
And she was there, my hope, my joy,
My own dear Genevieve!

She leant against the arméd man,
The statue of the arméd knight;
She stood and listened to my lay,
Amid the lingering light.

Few sorrows hath she of her own,
My hope! my joy! my Genevieve!
She loves me best, whene'er I sing
The songs that make her grieve.

I played a soft and doleful air,
I sang an old and moving story—
An old rude song, that suited well
   That ruin wild and hoary.

She listened with a flitting blush,
With downcast eyes and modest grace;
For well she knew, I could not choose
   But gaze upon her face.

I told her of the Knight that wore
Upon his shield a burning brand;
And that for ten long years he wooed
   The Lady of the Land.

I told her how he pined: and ah!
The deep, the low, the pleading tone
With which I sang another's love,
   Interpreted my own.

She listened with a flitting blush,
With downcast eyes, and modest grace;
And she forgave me, that I gazed
   Too fondly on her face!

But when I told the cruel scorn
That crazed that bold and lovely Knight,
And that he crossed the mountain-woods,
   Nor rested day nor night;

That sometimes from the savage den,
And sometimes from the darksome shade,
And sometimes starting up at once
   In green and sunny glade,—

There came and looked him in the face
An angel beautiful and bright;
And that he knew it was a Fiend,
    This miserable Knight!

And that unknowing what he did,
He leaped amid a murderous band,
And saved from outrage worse than death
    The Lady of the Land!

And how she wept, and clasped his knees;
And how she tended him in vain –
And ever strove to expiate
    The scorn that crazed his brain; –

And that she nursed him in a cave;
And how his madness went away,
When on the yellow forest-leaves
    A dying man he lay; –

His dying words – but when I reached
That tenderest strain of all the ditty,
My faultering voice and pausing harp
    Disturbed her soul with pity!

All impulses of soul and sense
Had thrilled my guileless Genevieve;
The music and the doleful tale,
    The rich and balmy eve;

And hopes, and fears that kindle hope,
An undistinguishable throng,
And gentle wishes long subdued,
    Subdued and cherished long!

> *She wept with pity and delight,*
> *She blushed with love, and virgin-shame;*
> *And like the murmur of a dream,*
> > *I heard her breathe my name.*

> *Her bosom heaved – she stepped aside,*
> *As conscious of my look she stepped –*
> *Then suddenly, with timorous eye*
> > *She fled to me and wept.*

> *She half enclosed me with her arms,*
> *She pressed me with a meek embrace;*
> *And bending back her head, looked up,*
> > *And gazed upon my face.*

> *'Twas partly love, and partly fear,*
> *And partly 'twas a bashful art,*
> *That I might rather feel, than see,*
> > *The swelling of her heart.*

> *I calmed her fears, and she was calm,*
> *And told her love with virgin pride;*
> *And so I won my Genevieve,*
> > *My bright and beauteous Bride.*

From Sockburn Coleridge returned – changed – to London. Back in the capital he took on a series of pieces of journalism, joining the staff of *The Morning Post*, writing copiously on politics, including some work as Parliamentary reporter, for its editor Daniel Stuart, to whom he had been introduced by Tom Wedgwood. He lived for a time at 21 Buckingham Street, off the Strand, where Sara and young Hartley had joined him; they enjoyed domestic life together briefly, but by March the strain in the relationship was showing again and Coleridge had moved out, this time to Charles Lamb's, in Islington; here, still taken by his German enthusiasm, Coleridge embarked on a translation of *Wallenstein*, the recent historical drama by Schiller.

Being in London allowed Coleridge to spend time with interesting contemporaries, such as the radical author William Godwin, and the chemist/inventor Humphry Davy, whom he had met at Bristol. But his London society, however exalted, could not compete with the call of his relationship with Wordsworth, and just as Wordsworth had travelled to Somerset three years earlier to be near Coleridge, now it was Coleridge's turn to follow his friend, heading north to meet him in April 1800.

Since December 1799 William and Dorothy had been at Town End cottage (now known as Dove Cottage), near Grasmere, just as they had planned on that walking tour from Sockburn earlier in the season; and it was to here that Coleridge travelled in the spring. The plan was originally just a quick visit to work on a second edition of the *Lyrical Ballads* (that there was commercial demand for this is revealing), but Coleridge quickly decided he wanted to bring his family up to settle here.

He found a suitable place to live in Keswick – some dozen miles from the Wordsworth home – and brought a very pregnant Sara and Hartley (and boxes and boxes of books) up in late June. By the end of July, they had arranged their affairs with one Mr Jackson, who was to be their new landlord, and they were in their new home, Greta Hall.

Greta Hall was – and remains – a large and elegant (though then barely finished) house beautifully situated on a little hill overlooking Keswick and the northern tip of Derwent Water. Dorothy wrote, shortly after visiting Greta Hall:

> His home is most delightfully situated, and combines all possible advantages both for his wife and himself. *She* likes to be near a town, *he* in the country. It is only half or a quarter of a mile from Keswick, and commands a view of the whole vale. Their little boy Hartley, who is an original sprite, is to come and stay with us…

When the Coleridges' next son was born on 14th September, he was named for his birthplace – Derwent Coleridge.

Greta Hall was where Part Two of 'Christabel' was completed; and this is where the surviving poem ends. More was certainly planned (the story is unfinished as we have it), and Coleridge even claimed in letters to have written much more (it stretched, he said, to some 1,400 lines, more than double the parts in evidence today). We can choose to believe him or not. In any case, 'Christabel' would never be accepted for inclusion in the *Lyrical Ballads* – and it's true, it hardly suited the collection's prevailing style. But then again, nor did 'The Ancient Mariner', hardly a poem of the simple life! And indeed, Wordsworth tried to remove the 'Mariner' from the new edition of the *Lyrical Ballads* – for while the first edition of the collection had received warm reviews, the long Coleridge poem which opened it had attracted much criticism.

This second edition of the *Lyrical Ballads* now in preparation would be more explicit than the first in its intentions, with a preface drafted by Wordsworth in September that expanded enormously on the old 'Advertisement' to produce a lengthy statement of belief and intent. Finally the 'Mariner' would remain in later editions of the collection, but with a little introduction to the poem written by Wordsworth making it clear that this one is *not* one of his, giving the poem some praise but also paying considerable attention to describing what he considers its 'great defects'. This 1800 edition would also see the first appearance in print of 'Love'.

As they had done at Somerset, the two poets walked back and forth between their houses, discussing their poetry, the *Lyrical Ballads*, and poetry in general.

The work these days wasn't all poetry, though, and Coleridge spent much of his time and energies exercised with philosophy. But his energies were not great – he was tired, and the damp brought on rheumatism (perhaps related to that childhood runaway episode?); to deal with it he took more laudanum, and more. If his use had ever been under control, it certainly was no longer now. The illnesses – particularly the rheumatic fevers – were especially bad in the early months of 1801, and the opium intake grew, and the dependency became graver and graver.

And – the happy birth of Derwent excepted – the always fragile marriage was finally coming apart at the seams. Sara Hutchinson was around a great deal, and Coleridge was torn (as so often) between his passion for her and his passionate certainty that his marriage was indissoluble. This, combined with the discomfort and the addiction, with nightmares and self-doubt, made for a wretched time.

Coleridge's feelings at this time are described in entries in his 'notebooks', a series of booklets of personal jottings, kept over years and years, which around this time suddenly become very exciting to explore. Where once they had been just collections of lists and useful data, now they have become a marvellous mixture of the brilliant and beautiful, the incredibly self-aware, the visionary, and the mundane, the dull, the repetitive... He records his dreams, he jots down lines of poetry or images that occur to him, he records accounts, observations, makes long lists of plant names (... Borage. Bottle moss. Box. Brakes. Bramble. Branks. Breakstone. Bromegrass. Brook lime. Brook weed. Broom...) and notes on German phonetics and philosophy. He writes with deep feeling of Asra, and other affecting matters, sometimes in other languages or encoded. During his Lakeland years, it is into these notebooks, and into his many long letters, that we find Coleridge's massive brainpower seeping – not in worked-through, fully realised and structured finished poems, but in what Richard Holmes has called 'a kind of glistening chaos'. Look, for example, at this entry, written on 19th October 1803:

Slanting Pillars of Light, like Ladders up to Heaven, their base always a field of vivid green Sunshine / – This is Oct.

19. 1803. Wed. Morn. tomorrow my Birth Day, 31 years of age! – O me! my very heart dies! –This *year* has been one painful Dream / I have done nothing! – O for God's sake, let me whip & spur, so that Christmas may not pass without some thing having been done / at all events to finish The Men & the Times, & to collect them & all my Newspaper essays into one Volume / to collect all my poems, finishing the Vision of the Maid of Orleans, ~~one~~ & the Dark Ladie, & make a second Volume / & to finish Christabel.– I ought too, in common gratitude, to write out my two Tours, for Sally Wedgwood/

Oct. 19. 1803. The general Fast Day – and all heart anxious concerning the Invasion. – A grey Day, windy – the vale, like a place in Faery, with the autumnal Colours, the orange, the red-brown, the crimson. the light yellow, the yet lingering Green, Beeches ~~all~~ & Birches, as they were blossoming Fire & Gold! – & the Sun in slanting pillars, or illuminated small parcels of mist, or single spots of softest greyish Light, now racing, now slowly gliding, now station-ary / – the mountains cloudy – the Lake has been a mirror so very clear, that the water became almost invisible – & now it rolls in white Breakers, like a Sea; & the wind snatches up the water, & drifts it like Snow / – and now the Rain Storm pelts against my Study window! – ~~Ο Σαρα Σαρα why am I~~ not happy! why have I not an unen-cumbered Heart! these beloved Books still before me, this noble Room, the very centre to which a whole world of beauty converges, the deep reservoir into which all these streams & currents of lovely Forms flow – my own mind so populous, so active, so full of noble schemes, so capable of realizing them / this heart so loving, so filled with noble affections – O ~~Ασρα~~! wherefore am I not happy! why for years have I not enjoyed one pure & sincere pleasure! – one full Joy! – one genuine Delight, that rings sharp to the Beat of the Finger! – † all cracked, & dull with base Alloy!

– Di Boni! mihi vim et virtutem / vel tu, [......], eheu! perdite amatio!

† But still have said to the poetic Feeling when it has awak'd in the Heart – Go! – come tomorrow. –

A day of Storm / at dinner an explosion of Temper from the Sisters / a dead Sleep after Dinner / the Rhubarb had its usual enfeebling-narcotic effect / I slept again with dreams of sorrow & pain, tho' not of downright Fright & prostration / I was worsted but not conquered – in sorrows and in sadness & in sore & angry Struggles – but not trampled down / but this will all come again, if I do not take care.

Storm all night – the wind scourging & lashing the rain, with the pauses of self-wearying Violence that returns to its wild work as if maddened by the necessity of the Pause / I, half-dozing, list'ning to the same, not without solicitations of the poetic Feeling / for from † I have written, Oct. 20. 1803, on Thursday Morning, 40 minutes past 2°clock.

So the Lake years continued. Coleridge walked up mountains with Wordsworth or alone (conquering Scafell Pike – England's highest mountain – alone in 1802); he received visitors, like the Lambs in the summer; he read a lot, and he wrote a lot.

A Thought Suggested by a
View of Saddleback in Cumberland

On stern Blencartha's perilous height
   The winds are tyrannous and strong;
And flashing forth unsteady light
From stern Blencathra's skiey height,
   As loud the torrents throng!
Beneath the moon, in gentle weather,

They bind the earth and sky together.
But oh! the sky and all its forms, how quiet!
The things that seek the earth, how full of noise and riot!

Coleridge's poetry-writing was getting harder, though, as his capacity to experience delight at the world was paling too. After a Christmas 1801 trip to London (where he took on more journalism work) and another trip early in 1802 to visit an ailing Asra at her new home at Gallow Hill, in Yorkshire, Coleridge returned to Greta Hall and sat down to write the finest poem in the language about the inability to write poetry.

Fuelled by his own personal troubles – his doubts about his writing, his unconsummated love for Asra and his miserable marriage to Sara, his ill health and his drug addiction, unsettling changes to his relationship with Wordsworth – he writes this verse-letter to Asra. In it he describes his anhedonia – his inability to experience pleasure – a chilling symptom of his depression, and in stark contrast to the heightened visions experienced in his opium dreams and preserved alive in 'Kubla Khan' and the 'Mariner'. This sad new poem would eventually be given the name 'Dejection: An Ode'.

Late, late yestreen I saw the new Moon,
With the old Moon in her arms;
And I fear, I fear, my Master dear!
We shall have a deadly storm.
Ballad of Sir Patrick Spence

I

Well! If the Bard was weather-wise, who made
The grand old ballad of Sir Patrick Spence,
This night, so tranquil now, will not go hence
Unroused by winds, that ply a busier trade

Than those which mould yon cloud in lazy flakes,
Or the dull sobbing draft, that moans and rakes
Upon the strings of this Æolian lute,
　　Which better far were mute.
　For lo! the New-moon winter-bright!
　And overspread with phantom light,
　(With swimming phantom light o'erspread
　But rimmed and circled by a silver thread)
I see the old Moon in her lap, foretelling
　The coming-on of rain and squally blast.
And oh! that even now the gust were swelling,
　And the slant night-shower driving loud and fast!
Those sounds which oft have raised me, whilst they awed,
　　And sent my soul abroad,
Might now perhaps their wonted impulse give,
Might startle this dull pain, and make it move and live!

II

A grief without a pang, void, dark, and drear,
　A stifled, drowsy, unimpassioned grief,
　Which finds no natural outlet, no relief,
　　In word, or sigh, or tear –
O Lady! in this wan and heartless mood,
To other thoughts by yonder throstle woo'd,
　All this long eve, so balmy and serene,
Have I been gazing on the western sky,
And its peculiar tint of yellow green:
And still I gaze – and with how blank an eye!
And those thin clouds above, in flakes and bars,
That give away their motion to the stars;
Those stars, that glide behind them or between,
Now sparkling, now bedimmed, but always seen:
Yon crescent Moon, as fixed as if it grew
In its own cloudless, starless lake of blue;

I see them all so excellently fair,
I see, not feel, how beautiful they are!

III

My genial spirits fail;
And what can these avail
To lift the smothering weight from off my breast?
It were a vain endeavour,
Though I should gaze for ever
On that green light that lingers in the west:
I may not hope from outward forms to win
The passion and the life, whose fountains are within.

IV

O Lady! we receive but what we give,
And in our life alone does Nature live:
Ours is her wedding-garment, ours her shroud!
And would we aught behold, of higher worth,
Than that inanimate cold world allowed
To the poor loveless ever-anxious crowd,
Ah! from the soul itself must issue forth
A light, a glory, a fair luminous cloud
Enveloping the Earth –
And from the soul itself must there be sent
A sweet and potent voice, of its own birth,
Of all sweet sounds the life and element!

V

O pure of heart! thou need'st not ask of me
What this strong music in the soul may be!
What, and wherein it doth exist,
This light, this glory, this fair luminous mist,
This beautiful and beauty-making power.

Joy, virtuous Lady! Joy that ne'er was given,
Save to the pure, and in their purest hour,
Life, and Life's effluence, cloud at once and shower,
Joy, Lady! is the spirit and the power,
Which wedding Nature to us gives in dower
    A new Earth and new Heaven,
Undreamt of by the sensual and the proud –
Joy is the sweet voice, Joy the luminous cloud –
      We in ourselves rejoice!
And thence flows all that charms or ear or sight,
All melodies the echoes of that voice,
All colours a suffusion from that light.

VI

There was a time when, though my path was rough,
    This joy within me dallied with distress,
And all misfortunes were but as the stuff
    Whence Fancy made me dreams of happiness:
For hope grew round me, like the twining vine,
And fruits, and foliage, not my own, seemed mine.
But now afflictions bow me down to earth:
Nor care I that they rob me of my mirth;
    But oh! each visitation
Suspends what nature gave me at my birth,
    My shaping spirit of Imagination.
For not to think of what I needs must feel,
    But to be still and patient, all I can;
And haply by abstruse research to steal
    From my own nature all the natural man –
This was my sole resource, my only plan:
Till that which suits a part infects the whole,
And now is almost grown the habit of my soul.

Hence, viper thoughts, that coil around my mind,
    Reality's dark dream!
I turn from you, and listen to the wind,
  Which long has raved unnoticed. What a scream
Of agony by torture lengthened out
That lute sent forth! Thou Wind, that rav'st without,
  Bare crag, or mountain-tairn, or blasted tree,
Or pine-grove whither woodman never clomb,
Or lonely house, long held the witches' home,
  Methinks were fitter instruments for thee,
Mad Lutanist! who in this month of showers,
Of dark-brown gardens, and of peeping flowers,
Mak'st Devils' yule, with worse than wintry song,
The blossoms, buds, and timorous leaves among.
  Thou Actor, perfect in all tragic sounds!
Thou mighty Poet, e'en to frenzy bold!
    What tell'st thou now about?
    'Tis of the rushing of an host in rout,
  With groans, of trampled men, with smarting wounds –
At once they groan with pain, and shudder with the cold!
But hush! there is a pause of deepest silence!
  And all that noise, as of a rushing crowd,
With groans, and tremulous shudderings – all is over –
  It tells another tale, with sounds less deep and loud!
    A tale of less affright,
    And tempered with delight,
As Otway's self had framed the tender lay, –
    'Tis of a little child
    Upon a lonesome wild,
Not far from home, but she hath lost her way:
And now moans low in bitter grief and fear,
And now screams loud, and hopes to make her mother hear.

'Tis midnight, but small thoughts have I of sleep:
Full seldom may my friend such vigils keep!
Visit her, gentle Sleep! with wings of healing,
    And may this storm be but a mountain-birth,
May all the stars hang bright above her dwelling,
        Silent as though they watched the sleeping Earth!
            With light heart may she rise,
            Gay fancy, cheerful eyes,
        Joy lift her spirit, joy attune her voice;
To her may all things live, from pole to pole,
Their life the eddying of her living soul!
        O simple spirit, guided from above,
Dear Lady! friend devoutest of my choice,
Thus mayest thou ever, evermore rejoice.

This poem – much shortened and now addressed to Wordsworth instead of Asra – was published in *The Morning Post* on 4th October. It was the same day that his friend married Mary Hutchinson. (And Coleridge, most conspicuously, did not marry her sister.) Rather pointedly, this date was also his own seventh wedding anniversary with that other Sara, née Fricker.

Another Coleridge baby was born in December, a daughter, who was christened Sara after her mother. (And not, presumably, after the woman her father was in love with.) The next year her father followed 'Dejection' with another powerful poem of his own miserable situation, 'The Pains of Sleep', evoking the terrorising of his opium-withdrawal nightmares.

That summer, the summer of 1803, the old trio of Coleridge, Wordsworth and Dorothy were off on a walking tour again – Mary, being unwell, stayed at home – this time to the Trossachs, mid-Scotland. Coleridge split off from the Wordsworths early in the trip, then alone walked more than 250 miles in eight gruelling days, to Perth. On the way, at Fort Augustus, he was arrested briefly as a spy.

It was during this Scottish absence that Southey returned to the picture; he and his wife Edith (Sara Coleridge's sister) arrived at Greta Hall. They were still there when Coleridge returned in mid-September. And they were there to stay. It would be at Greta Hall that Southey would breathe his last, forty years later.

In the hope of getting over his illness – which in turn would allow him to reduce his opium-taking – Coleridge made plans to move again, from the dampness of the Lakes to a drier climate. He left his family at Greta Hall, in Southey's care, in mid-January. By March he had booked a sea passage, boarding the *Speedwell* at Portsmouth on 6th April. On 9th April the *Speedwell* set sail, bound for Malta.

After a grim sea voyage, in which Coleridge was beset by illness (eye troubles especially, as well as the usual opium-related intestinal problems), and pursued by nightmares from which he would awake to find his pillows soaked with tears, the *Speedwell* drew in to Malta, at last, on Friday 18th May. Coleridge was thirty-one, and struggling; he may have been a genius, with massive talent and potential, but he was unhappily married, he was constantly ill, he was desperately conflicted in his beliefs and his passions, he was broke, and a drug addict with little prospect of recovery.

The money problem, at least, was more easily fixed than most, and Coleridge was soon earning a salary employed as private secretary, then acting Public Secretary, to the High Commissioner, Sir Alexander Ball. It was an unusual and fascinating time to be in Malta – especially in the service of the Crown – as the island had only very recently been won by England from the occupying French. (An interesting *choice* of destination, then.) But he would find Malta an isolating experience, and wrote almost no letters home during his time there.

An Exile

Friend, Lover, Husband, Sister, Brother!
Dear names close in upon each other!
Alas! poor Fancy's bitter-sweet –
Our names, and but our names can meet.

Though depressed and isolated, Coleridge managed to travel
a little, spending his autumn in Sicily, climbing Mount Etna, and
continuing to make copious Notebook notes.

He had already begun to doubt whether he ought to be staying in Malta, when a tragedy struck that made his mind up
for him. Wordsworth's younger brother John was captain of the
Abergavenny; in late March of 1805 Coleridge received news in
Malta that the *Abergavenny* had sunk off Weymouth and John
had died.

Coleridge had been very fond of John Wordsworth, and was
deeply upset at the news – all the more, perhaps, because he had
considered John a possible match for his beloved Asra – and,
dispirited by the Malta experience in general, he began to plan his
return. The new setting hadn't done much to help curb his addiction anyway, nor his ill health, and absence had not made Asra
retreat an inch in his affections, so there was little reason to stay.
He was somewhat delayed waiting for a permanent replacement
to fill his post, but the moment the new Public Secretary arrived
in September he was off. He left Malta on the 23rd.

The voyage down from Portsmouth had been so disagreeable
that for his return Coleridge plotted a route that involved covering as much of the distance as possible over land. So first he
would return to Sicily, thence to Naples and then overland up
through Italy and northern Europe. It didn't quite go according
to plan, however.

The first problem was Rome, where he was unexpectedly
delayed, or rather, where he delayed himself, having befriended

Ludwig Tieck, with whom he discussed Goethe, and a group of painters including the young American Washington Allston, and George Wallis with whose family he boarded temporarily when his funds ran dry. And then, having been unexpectedly delayed in Rome, he was unexpectedly rushed out of it in May when Napoleon (newly occupying the city) ordered all Britons to leave. Coleridge's route then took him to Pisa, and thence to Livorno (a few years later and he would have found Shelley and Byron here together), where he pretended to be American. At last – more war and politics precluding the much-desired land crossing – he set sail from Livorno on 23rd June 1806.

The journey home on the *Gosport* was every bit as bad as the outbound sailing had been, and much longer. He was seasick for the first time in his life (on the crossing to Germany with John Chester and the Wordsworths he had been amused to find himself the only one unafflicted); he was constipated, his stomach was a dreadful state – and on one occasion they were even boarded by a privateer. He landed – gratefully – in Kent on 11th August. Meeting him for the first time after his return, a concerned Dorothy Wordsworth would comment, 'Never did I feel such a shock as the first in sight of him… He is utterly changed; and yet sometimes, when he was in animated conversation concerning things removed from him, I saw something of his former self…'

Back in London Coleridge chose not to hasten up to Keswick to visit his estranged wife and beloved children, nor even to write to them. Indeed, he avoided most of his friends – in part shamed by his unheroic return, perhaps? But he was soon back in contact with Daniel Stuart, his old editor from *The Morning Post*, and settled to live in the offices of Stuart's *Courier*, planning further lectures; and took advantage of being back home to rekindle one of his great pleasures, the friendship of William and Dorothy. He had planned, in fact, to make his way without them, starting his new life of journalism, writing, lecturing and order, free of the ties from his former life (and without a wife), but his most intimate friends would not stay out of his life for long, and with them came a powerful draw away from the controlled existence he had planned for London.

The Wordsworths were wintering at a farmhouse at Coleorton, in Leicestershire – a house belonging to Sir George Beaumont – and late in 1806 (after a brief and reluctant visit to Sara) Coleridge and his son Hartley went to stay with them for a spell. William's sister-in-law Sara – Asra – was staying with them too, which as usual was simultaneously a thrill and a torment.

Wordsworth had been keeping busy since Coleridge had seen him last; his greatest work had been the completion of the 13-book version of the autobiographical poem that would come to be called *The Prelude*. Now, though, it was still called 'Poem to Coleridge'. At the start of January Wordsworth read the poem to its dedicatee, who – overwhelmed – responded with this enthusiastic praise, heartfelt but full of doubt of his own gifts, shame at his own failings to write great things:

To William Wordsworth
[Composed on the night after his recitation
of a poem on the growth of an individual mind.]

Friend of the wise! and Teacher of the Good!
Into my heart have I received that Lay
More than historic, that prophetic Lay
Wherein (high theme by thee first sung aright)
Of the foundations and the building up
Of a Human Spirit thou hast dared to tell
What may be told, to the understanding mind
Revealable; and what within the mind
By vital breathings secret as the soul
Of vernal growth, oft quickens in the heart
Thoughts all too deep for words!—

Theme hard as high!
Of smiles spontaneous, and mysterious fears
(The first-born they of Reason and twin-birth),
Of tides obedient to external force,
And currents self-determined, as might seem,
Or by some inner Power; of moments awful,
Now in thy inner life, and now abroad,
When power streamed from thee, and thy soul received
The light reflected, as a light bestowed –
Of fancies fair, and milder hours of youth,
Hyblean murmurs of poetic thought
Industrious in its joy, in vales and glens
Native or outland, lakes and famous hills!
Or on the lonely high-road, when the stars
Were rising; or by secret mountain-streams,
The guides and the companions of thy way!

Of more than Fancy, of the Social Sense
Distending wide, and man beloved as man,
Where France in all her towns lay vibrating
Like some becalméd bark beneath the burst
Of Heaven's immediate thunder, when no cloud
Is visible, or shadow on the main.
For thou wert there, thine own brows garlanded,
Amid the tremor of a realm aglow,
Amid a mighty nation jubilant,
When from the general heart of human kind
Hope sprang forth like a full-born Deity!
——Of that dear Hope afflicted and struck down,
So summoned homeward, thenceforth calm and sure
From the dread watch-tower of man's absolute self,
With light unwaning on her eyes, to look
Far on – herself a glory to behold,
The Angel of the vision! Then (last strain)
Of Duty, chosen Laws controlling choice,

Action and joy! – An Orphic song indeed,
A song divine of high and passionate thoughts
To their own music chaunted!

                        O great Bard!
Ere yet that last strain dying awed the air,
With steadfast eye I viewed thee in the choir
Of ever-enduring men. The truly great
Have all one age, and from one visible space
Shed influence! They, both in power and act,
Are permanent, and Time is not with them,
Save as it worketh for them, they in it.
Nor less a sacred Roll, than those of old,
And to be placed, as they, with gradual fame
Among the archives of mankind, thy work
Makes audible a linkéd lay of Truth,
Of Truth profound a sweet continuous lay,
Not learnt, but native, her own natural notes!
Ah! as I listened with a heart forlorn,
The pulses of my being beat anew:
And even as life returns upon the drowned,
Life's joy rekindling roused a throng of pains –
Keen pangs of Love, awakening as a babe
Turbulent, with an outcry in the heart;
And fears self-willed, that shunned the eye of Hope;
And Hope that scarce would know itself from Fear;
Sense of past Youth, and Manhood come in vain,
And Genius given, and Knowledge won in vain;
And all which I had culled in wood-walks wild,
And all which patient toil had reared, and all,
Commune with thee had opened out – but flowers
Strewed on my corse, and borne upon my bier,
In the same coffin, for the self-same grave!

That way no more! and ill beseems it me,
Who came a welcomer in herald's guise,
Singing of Glory, and Futurity,
To wander back on such unhealthful road,
Plucking the poisons of self-harm! And ill
Such intertwine beseems triumphal wreaths
Strew'd before thy advancing!

                        Nor do thou,
Sage Bard! impair the memory of that hour
Of thy communion with my nobler mind
By pity or grief, already felt too long!
Nor let my words import more blame than needs.
The tumult rose and ceased: for Peace is nigh
Where wisdom's voice has found a listening heart.
Amid the howl of more than wintry storms,
The Halcyon hears the voice of vernal hours
Already on the wing.

                        Eve following eve,
Dear tranquil time, when the sweet sense of Home
Is sweetest! moments for their own sake hailed
And more desired, more precious, for thy song,
In silence listening like a devout child,
My soul lay passive, by thy various strain
Driven as in surges now beneath the stars,
With momentary stars of my own birth,
Fair constellated foam, still darting off
Into the darkness; now a tranquil sea,
Outspread and bright, yet swelling to the moon.

And when – O Friend! my comforter and guide!
Strong in thyself, and powerful to give strength! –
Thy long sustainéd Song finally closed,
And thy deep voice had ceased – yet thou thyself

Wert still before my eyes, and round us both
That happy vision of belovéd faces –
Scarce conscious, and yet conscious of its close
I sate, my being blended in one thought
(Thought was it? or aspiration? or resolve?)
Absorbed, yet hanging still upon the sound –
And when I rose, I found myself in prayer.

Shapes and thoughts that tortured me…

from **Recollections of Love**

I

How warm this woodland wild Recess!
Love surely hath been breathing here;
And this sweet bed of heath, my dear!
Swells up, then sinks with faint caress,
As if to have you yet more near.

II

Eight springs have flown, since last I lay
On sea-ward Quantock's heathy hills,
Where quiet sounds from hidden rills
Float here and there, like things astray,
And high o'er head the sky-lark shrills.

III

No voice as yet had made the air
Be music with your name; yet why
That asking look? that yearning sigh?
That sense of promise every where?
Belovéd! flew your spirit by?…

This summer – 1807 – Coleridge travelled *en famille* with Sara and the children to stay with Thomas Poole, though this was hardly the high-point of their marriage and there were plans to separate already in mind... (When the time finally came for the separation, Coleridge's pious brother George would disapprove. Another rift with his Ottery family.)

This trip west gave Coleridge a good opportunity to spend time with the faithful Poole, but also allowed him to meet a new friend, Thomas de Quincey. De Quincey had come from London to Nether Stowey in the hope of finding Coleridge at Poole's, but only eventually caught up with him at Bridgwater, where the two men talked through the night about opium addiction. (By which I really mean – as any friend of Coleridge might have predicted – that de Quincey listened while Coleridge did the talking-through-the-night himself.) Fourteen years later de Quincey would write his most famous work, *Confessions of an English Opium-Eater* in which he anatomised his own addicted relationship with the drug.

Coleridge's addiction was bad this year (he was taking up to two quarts a week), and his marriage was even worse; soon he and Sara would separate, and Coleridge would fall ill. His attendant nurses were the Morgan family, who took him in and looked after him through his illness. John Morgan had been an old schoolfellow of Coleridge's at Christ's Hospital, from a family of Bristol Unitarians, who now lived (in Bristol's St James's Square) with his wife and sister-in-law, and who resumed this friendship just in time to take Coleridge in for this troubled spell. This particular period of residence, so typical of Coleridge ('All his cuckoo-like propensities were at once aroused...' writes Richard Holmes) would only last a few weeks, but it would not be the last time the understanding Morgan and his family would be called upon to provide succour for their increasingly fragile friend.

Coleridge had long been planning a series of lectures in London, and while his illness didn't require the plans to be put on hold it certainly meant that his performances were rather less regular and less consistent than they might have been. He was speaking at the Royal Institution (organised by Humphry Davy), a series of eighteen lectures. At his best he was magnificent, but the lectures were erratic too; even when in fine health Coleridge was prone to unreliability, inconsistency, and he was often rambling and unprepared in these days when illness and opium struggles were simply too strong for him. In his lectures this season he spoke on 'Poetry and the Principles of Taste' (Keats and Byron were among his audience), on drama, on art, on education. They were sometimes inspired, sometimes controversial. They exercised his brain, entertained it, and kept it – and him – busy, and productive.

After part of summer 1808 at Bury St Edmund's with his Quaker friends the Clarksons, Coleridge made another trip up to the Lake District. Since May the Wordsworths had been in a larger house, Allan Bank, and it was here that Coleridge came to spend the winter, and as was his habit ended up staying a year and a half. (De Quincey spent the winter holed up in Allan Bank too, then in the spring of 1809 moved into the Wordsworths' old home, Dove Cottage, where he would live for ten years.) From Allan Bank Coleridge could easily visit his children, and with Sara Hutchinson could work on his new scheme: *The Friend*.

Wordsworth had grave doubts about Coleridge's ability to pull this new project off, writing to Thomas Poole in May:

I gave it to you as my deliberate opinion, formed upon proofs which have been strengthening for years, that he neither will nor can execute any thing of important benefit either to himself his family or mankind. Neither his talents nor his genius mighty as they are nor his vast information will avail him anything; they are all frustrated by a derangement in his intellectual and moral constitution – In fact he has no voluntary power of mind whatsoever, nor is he capable of acting under any *constraint* of duty or moral obligation. Do not suppose that I mean to say that The Friend may not appear – it may – but it cannot go on for any length of time. I am *sure* it cannot.

The Friend was never likely to be a tremendous success, but it would, at least, be sustained longer than *The Watchman* had managed. It too was to be a journal, in this case written largely – sometimes almost exclusively – by Coleridge himself, dealing with political theory and philosophy. (But containing other things too – pieces written by other hands would include never-before-published parts of the Wordsworth poem that would become *The Prelude*.) It was often dense, and was often very poorly received, but its high points are moments of great thoughtful clarity. With Asra's help, the first issue was ready to appear in the summer of 1809. Coleridge walked the thirty-something miles to Penrith to have it printed – as he would have to do for every issue – and it appeared on 1st June. The first issue, wrote Coleridge, 'bears marks of the effort and anxiety with which it was written, and is composed less happily than I could wish…'.

On 4th November 1809, Coleridge's mother died at Ottery, after an excruciatingly painful illness. He did not travel down to visit her in her last days, nor to attend her funeral.

And in March 1810, *The Friend* reached its twenty-eighth, and final, issue.

It was inevitable. Things were changing at Allan Bank, and from Coleridge's perspective at least they were not changing for the better. The happy group was coming apart, and *The Friend* was only the first casualty. The beloved Asra, who had assisted Coleridge in his work, was leaving, travelling down to her brother Tom's farm in Wales; more catastrophic even than this, Coleridge and Wordsworth were about to have an argument from which their friendship would never really recover.

After some discomfort in the Allan Bank household, Coleridge passed a period at Greta Hall, spending time with his children, teaching young Sara Italian; then he headed south – London-wards – with Basil Montagu, a friend of Wordsworth's, who dropped a bombshell in casual conversation. Apparently, said Montagu, the Wordsworths considered Coleridge an 'absolute nuisance' and a 'rotten drunkard'. There was no one in the world whose good opinion mattered more to Coleridge than Wordsworth's, and he was hurt, irreparably.

Back down in London, distraught and betrayed, Coleridge took rooms at the Hudson Hotel on King Street, Covent Garden and – with neither Asra nor Wordsworth in his life now – began to drink a great deal. Charles Lamb tried to make light of the problem, describing Coleridge in a letter to Dorothy as looking:

> … like Bacchus, Bacchus ever sleek and young. He is going to turn sober, but his Clock has not struck yet, meantime he pours down goblet after goblet, the 2d to see where the 1st is gone, the 3d to see no harm happens to the second, a fourth to say there's another coming, and a 5th to say he's not sure he's the last.

The years that followed, spent mostly in London, were perhaps the darkest of Coleridge's life. Living mainly back at the Morgans' (who did all they could to rescue him and draw him up from his lowest ebbs) on Portland Place in Hammersmith village, he went through suicidal phases, often unable to work (though still promising much), suffering gruesome nightmares which he recorded in agonised entries in his Notebooks, brooding on his state and failing (yet again) to come to terms with – let alone cure himself of – his addiction. At some of the worst moments he would escape to London, and long-suffering John Morgan would pursue him and drag him back into the Hammersmith household.

Some of the work that Coleridge did manage to complete in this time, mainly further series of lectures and large amounts of journalism for *The Courier*, was of significant value, however. He spoke at the Philosophical Institution on Fetter Lane, Fleet Street, for a course of lectures that ran through the 1811–12 winter; his subjects included Milton, and 'the Principles of Poetry', but it was the lectures on Shakespeare that were – and remain –

the most important. Particularly notable is lecture number twelve, delivered on 2nd January, his study of another great waverer – to whom he compared himself: Hamlet.

Influenced by his reading of Schlegel, Coleridge's lecture on *Hamlet* dramatically altered how the play was perceived, affecting our understanding of it even today. In the eighteenth century *Hamlet* had been dismissed (misunderstood) by Dr Johnson and Voltaire, but Coleridge rescued it, offering a sympathetic study of a character's psychology, in particular the workings of his introspective mind. In the process he offered (no less) an original insight into the previously unrecognised genius of Shakespeare.

Overall the Shakespeare lectures had ample moments of brilliance, and many ideas that would transform habits of literary criticism. They were a success. 'They have been brilliant,' wrote Crabb Robinson, who then qualified the praise with, 'that is, in passages.'

Yes, the Shakespeare lectures did indeed have passages of original brilliance; but they also (towards the end of the series) included passages lifted from Schlegel's Shakespearean criticism, sometimes word for word. Coleridge would face accusations of plagiarism now – as he would at other points in his career – where his borrowing from the works of various German writers was overly enthusiastic and unacknowledged. These tend not to be wholesale liftings of someone else's ideas – or rather, when he lifts their ideas he also develops them, expands them, leaving some of his works a sort of patchwork of writings (his and other people's) in creative exchange with one another. In a fair summation of the evidence, Richard Holmes concludes elegantly, 'One can say that Coleridge plagiarised, but that no one plagiarised like Coleridge.'

In a visit up to the Lakes (his last) in the spring of 1812 to arrange a reprinting of *The Friend*, Coleridge's coach passed through Grasmere without stopping to visit Wordsworth. The next month Wordsworth came down to London to see him, in the hope of a reconciliation, which Crabb Robinson helped to broker. When Coleridge gave his summer lectures on drama in May, Wordsworth attended some of them. The friends were speaking again, but it was not as it had been before, in the days when Wordsworth had followed Coleridge to Somerset, or Coleridge had followed Wordsworth to the Lakes, in order to inspire each other, to focus and challenge each other's unique creative potential.

This sadly lost friendship was far from Coleridge's only trouble this year, though. Money worries were becoming worse, with the annuity he had been relying on from the Wedgwoods now at risk. Thomas Wedgwood had died while Coleridge was on his Maltese adventure and his half of the annuity was secure and being paid regularly to Coleridge's wife, but Josiah was having trouble affording his half now. The only solution for Coleridge was work, and to throw himself on the mercy of other friends; he spent the winter lecturing at the Surrey Institute, and living with the Morgans again. This time his stay in their house – at 17 Berners Street, in Marylebone – lasted a year and a half.

Coleridge's work in 1812 wasn't all lectures and journalism; he was certainly far from idle; and among other things to show for his efforts, he saw his play *Remorse* premiere at Drury Lane in January 1813. In this work, a retitled version of his old *Osorio*, Inquisition Spain was the backdrop for a rather Gothic blank-verse melodrama of brothers who are rivals for love. It was – rather unusually for Coleridge's work at first appearance – well received.

Life at the Morgans' could have been more restful; in 1813 John Morgan himself fell ill, and subsequently went bankrupt and was forced to flee to Ireland to escape his creditors. Coleridge, who had entered the household as their charity-case friend, emotionally needy, dependent and broke, was now left to take charge of the welfare of suddenly impoverished women of the household, Mary Morgan and her lovely sister, Charlotte Brent and – rather surprisingly – he did just that. In December he placed the two women in rooms at Ashley in Wiltshire. This season he spent a fair bit of time around there himself, too. Based at Bristol now, he lectured on Shakespeare.

While in the area, staying in Bath, Coleridge suddenly fell apart. Walking home from Ashley to his rooms at the Grey Hound Inn, he collapsed with what seems to have been a psychological crisis – a crisis of faith, of opium guilt, a spiritual meltdown of many kinds at once. But some good came of this; by the time he had recovered his equilibrium – and his faith – he was also ready to admit his opium problems, and sought professional help, putting himself in the care of Dr Daniel at Bristol. Coleridge was lodged at 2 Queen's Square, where he was under permanent watch – all sharp objects removed from his room – and Dr Daniel began gradually to reduce the addict's dosage.

By the autumn Coleridge had escaped back to the Morgans', first at Ashley, then Calne in Wiltshire; and the worst of the crisis over, he was writing again. He was beginning to assemble his poems for a collected edition, and there were two major projects that left the blocks around now, one of which would not come to much, the other which would be among the greatest pieces of his legacy.

Coleridge corresponded with the distinguished publisher John Murray (publisher of Byron and Scott) about the possibility of his embarking on a translation of Goethe's *Faust*. Who better to undertake such a task than this brilliant Germanophile with a taste and a knack for the supernatural? Shelley, who attempted passages of *Faust* himself, commented that only Coleridge could ever really do it justice. Coleridge may have been eager to set off, but Murray was cooler, and as far as we know, regrettably, no progress was ever made. Certainly Coleridge would deny that he had ever put pen to paper. Except that in 1820

Goethe himself wrote that Coleridge had completed a good deal of it, and he surely may have known what he was talking about. Just recently, 2007 saw the publication of an English-language verse *Faust* claiming to be Coleridge's translation, apparently first published in 1821 but for some reason anonymously; while it may indeed be the work that it claims to be, we might also never know with certainty. What we can be sure of is that whatever attention Coleridge may have settled on this project at this point, it certainly wasn't a full-time occupation – he had plenty of other big professional challenges occupying his literary talents and protean intelligence.

He wrote the prose commentary to the '*Ancient Mariner*' – a narrative gloss which runs alongside almost every edition of the poem published today; and an essay on criticism inspired by his reading of Kant; and a preface to the new edition of his poems, a preface which over the course of the summer would grow into Coleridge's most important piece of prose critical thinking, *Biographia Literaria*. This would be some time yet in the writing, though…

But first, April 1816 saw two events, falling in the space of a few days, that would help to define the rest of Coleridge's life and his literary reputation: moving house, and meeting a fellow-poet, George Gordon, Lord Byron. The impact of the meeting with young Byron may be less obvious, as they would never be good friends, indeed would never meet again after this single encounter as Byron was within the month about to leave the country for good; but it did have one significant influence. It was Byron who persuaded Coleridge to recite 'Kubla Khan' to him, and persuaded him that it needed to be published; 'Christabel', about which Byron had written admiringly to Coleridge the previous autumn, ought to be published too. This meeting was on Wednesday 10th April; on the morning of the Friday, 12th April, Byron's publisher John Murray visited Coleridge and declared himself willing to undertake their publication.

Duly a volume appeared in May, *Christabel and Other Poems*; in it were both 'Christabel' (its two parts) and 'Kubla Khan', and another old piece which would counteract any apparent glamorising of opium use that readers might find in the story of 'Kubla Khan''s genesis. Yes, you may think laudanum is fun, that it frees your imagination and allows you to access new levels of your creative self – but here's what it's also like:

The Pains of Sleep

Ere on my bed my limbs I lay,
It hath not been my use to pray
With moving lips or bended knees;
But silently, by slow degrees,
My spirit I to Love compose,
In humble trust mine eye-lids close,
With reverential resignation,
No wish conceived, no thought exprest,
Only a sense of supplication;
A sense o'er all my soul imprest
That I am weak, yet not unblest,
Since in me, round me, every where
Eternal Strength and Wisdom are.

But yester-night I prayed aloud
In anguish and in agony,
Up-starting from the fiendish crowd
Of shapes and thoughts that tortured me:
A lurid light, a trampling throng,
Sense of intolerable wrong,
And whom I scorned, those only strong!
Thirst of revenge, the powerless will
Still baffled, and yet burning still!
Desire with loathing strangely mixed

On wild or hateful objects fixed.
Fantastic passions! maddening brawl!
And shame and terror over all!
Deeds to be hid which were not hid,
Which all confused I could not know
Whether I suffered, or I did:
For all seemed guilt, remorse or woe,
My own or others still the same
Life-stifling fear, soul-stifling shame.

So two nights passed: the night's dismay
Saddened and stunned the coming day.
Sleep, the wide blessing, seemed to me
Distemper's worst calamity.
The third night, when my own loud scream
Had waked me from the fiendish dream,
O'ercome with sufferings strange and wild,
I wept as I had been a child;
And having thus by tears subdued
My anguish to a milder mood,
Such punishments, I said, were due
To natures deepliest stained with sin,–
For aye entempesting anew
The unfathomable hell within,
The horror of their deeds to view,
To know and loathe, yet wish and do!
Such griefs with such men well agree,
But wherefore, wherefore fall on me?
To be beloved is all I need,
And whom I love, I love indeed.

Christabel and Other Poems was poorly received. But someone must have found something of merit in the collection; it was reprinted twice within the year.

James Gillman, a young surgeon, lived with his wife Ann and their family at Moreton House, South Grove in Highgate village, just north of London; Coleridge visited the young doctor on the afternoon of 12th April (the day he and Murray had agreed the publication of the *Christabel* volume) and by the Monday he had moved into the Gillmans' house, in the hope that the doctor's attentions would help him to wean himself off his addiction by controlling his supply. He planned to stay a month. When the Gillmans moved, in 1823, to nearby 3 The Grove, Coleridge moved with them, to a house where he would remain for more than a decade, and which would be his last home. Though his work had been poorly received by the critics, this portly middle-aged poet-philosopher-visionary-addict had more than his share of ardent young admirers too, who would come to the Highgate house, usually on Thursdays, to sit and listen to his wisdom. His distinguished roll-call of visitors included John Stuart Mill, James Fenimore Cooper, Ralph Waldo Emerson, and Thomas Carlyle, who described him as 'the sage of Highgate'.

Coleridge's capacity to speak had not dimmed with age. 'Zounds!' remarked one man foolish enough to try and argue with him, 'I was never so bethumped with words.' (This line, incidentally, was reported by another man present at the 'discussion' – Walter Scott.) And Coleridge – always strong on self-awareness – recognised that he was prone to what he called 'oneversazioni'… Some of his sparkling monologues were transcribed – by admirers like his nephew Henry Nelson Coleridge – and captured for posthumous publication as his *Table Talk*.

Lamb came to visit him that first Highgate summer, and heard him read; he wrote to Wordsworth, '[Coleridge] is at present under the medical care of a Mr Gilman (Killman?) a Highgate Apothecary, where he plays at leaving off Laudanum. I think him essentially not touched: he is very bad, but then he wonderfully picks up another day, and his face when he repeats his verses hath its ancient glory, an Archangel a little damaged.'

Youth's no longer here...

The latter half of Coleridge's life – especially the final eighteen years spent with the Gillmans in Highgate, are frequently written off as an example of wasted potential, a great creative genius failing to create, a mid-life burn-out, but the truth is quite different. Yes, it is true that his poetry never matched the dazzling burst that produced such astonishing work in those few months in 1797–8; but even in his latter years he remained prolific, and brilliant, albeit in different forms. His last two decades were not the life of a visionary genius poet, perhaps, but he was a prose writer and political philosopher and literary critic and theological thinker of incredible talents. The poetry is replaced by lectures and essays, pamphlets and newspaper articles, by the writing in his notebooks, his letters and very much more.

At the Gillmans' Coleridge started on a piece of work dealing with big subjects including moral responsibility, which would be published in two parts as his *Lay Sermons*. The first part appeared in December 1816, the second in the following April. Then in July came *Sibylline Leaves*, his first edition of collected poems; and a 'dramatic entertainment' called *Zapolya: a Christian Tale* (which he wasn't able to persuade either of the principal London theatres to stage); and (also in this incredibly productive year) *Biographia Literaria*.

Biographia Literaria is a sort of autobiographical-philosophical-literary-critical meditation, apparently quite chaotically structured (as the reviewers were quick to point out) but ambitious in scope and filled with what would become very influential ideas.

The twenty-two chapters are split into two parts, the first being the more autobiographical (friendships with the other poets, his German influences, etc.) but also introducing in Chapter IV his now famous distinction between 'Imagination' (more active, alive, linked to the divine) and 'Fancy' (which operates with 'fixities and definites'); the second part being an exploration of literary language, poetic metre and form, the work of writers including Shakespeare, Milton, Chaucer and Herbert, and a substantial critical response to Wordsworth's poetry and his *Lyrical Ballads* Preface with its notion of a 'natural' language to be found among the lower social classes:

> During the first year that Mr Wordsworth and I were neighbours our conversations turned frequently on the two cardinal points of poetry, the power of exciting the sympathy of the reader by a faithful adherence to the truth of nature, and the power of giving the interest of novelty by the modifying colours of imagination... The thought suggested itself (to which of us I do not recollect) that a series of poems might be composed of two sorts. In the one, the incidents and agents were to be, in part at least, supernatural... For the second class, subjects were to be chosen from ordinary life...
>
> As far... as Mr Wordsworth in his preface contended, and most ably contended, for a reformation in our poetic diction, as far as he has evinced the truth of passion, and the dramatic propriety of those figures and metaphors in the original poets which, stript of their justifying reasons and converted into mere artifices of connection or ornament, constitute the characteristic falsity in the poetic style of the moderns; and as far as he has, with equal acuteness and clearness, pointed out the process by which this

change was effected and the resemblances between that state into which the reader's mind is thrown by the pleasurable confusion of thought from an unaccustomed train of words and images and that state which is induced by the natural language of impassioned feeling, he undertook a useful task and deserves all praise, both for the attempt and for the execution...

My own differences from certain supposed parts of Mr Wordsworth's theory ground themselves on the assumption that his words had been rightly interpreted, as purporting that the proper diction for poetry in general consists altogether in a language taken, with due exceptions, from the mouths of men in real life, a language which actually constitutes the natural conversation of the men under the influence of natural feelings. My objection is, first, that in any sense this rule is applicable only to certain classes of poetry; secondly, that even to these classes it is not applicable, except in such a sense as hath never by any one (as far as I know or have read) been denied or doubted; and, lastly, that as far as, or in that degree in which it is practicable, it is yet as a *rule* useless, if not injurious, and therefore either need not or ought not to be practised...

Schelling, Kant and Fichte feature in a chapter on philosophy in Part I. (Schelling's own writing is 'borrowed' at some length, too.) There's also a lot of David Hartley in places. Another chapter is billed as 'An affectionate exhortation to those who in early life feel themselves disposed to become authors'. Chapter XIV includes the famous quotation about 'the willing suspension of disbelief' (which is what allows us, for example, to enjoy fiction, temporarily accepting as true things that we know really aren't). Not bad for something originally intended merely as an explanatory preface to *Sibylline Leaves*...

Among the *Biographia*'s first readers, and admirers, were John Keats and Percy Bysshe Shelley. But the reviews were bad, in particular a cruel (and brilliant) attack from Hazlitt in *The Edinburgh Review*, in which he describes the author of *Biographia*:

> … playing at hawk and buzzard between sense and nonsense, — floating or sinking in fine Kantean categories, in a state of suspended animation 'twixt dreaming and awake, — quitting the plain ground of "history and particular facts" for the first butterfly theory, fancy-bred from the maggots of his brain, — going up in an air-balloon filled with fetid gas from the writings of Jacob Behmen and the mystics, and coming down in a parachute made of the soiled and fashionable leaves of the Morning Post, — promising us an account of the Intellectual System of the Universe, and putting us off with a reference to a promised dissertation on the Logos, introductory to an intended commentary on the entire Gospel of St. John.
>
> … If it is the proper business of the philosopher to dream over theories, and to neglect or gloss over facts, to fit them to his theories or his conscience; we confess we know of few writers, ancient or modern, who have come nearer to the perfection of this character than the author before us.
>
> After a desultory and unsatisfactory attempt (Chap. II.) to account for and disprove the common notion of the irritability of authors, Mr. Coleridge proceeds (by what connexion we know not) to a full, true and particular account of the personal, domestic, and literary habits of his friend Mr. Southey, — to all which we have but one objection, namely, that it seems quite unnecessary, as we never heard them impugned…

And so it goes on. For a little over eleven thousand words. (That is, more than half the length of this biography.)

Leigh Hunt commented, 'O ye critics, the best of ye, what havoc does personal difference play with your judgments!'

Apart from the occasional seaside holiday, Coleridge – who had spent so many restless years – didn't stray much from London any more. It was here that he resumed his acquaintance in summer 1817 with Ludwig Tieck, whom he'd first met in Rome and who was now on a research trip to England. It was here in London that Coleridge resumed his role as lecturer, speaking over the winter at the London Philosophical Society on comparative literature, and European writers in particular. (Hazlitt, meanwhile, was giving a rival lecture series just down the road.) And it was here that he met up again with Wordsworth, a meeting even cooler than the previous one had been; though as Wordsworth had at the very least leafed through his old friend's new book (which argued with him, and criticised him, quite explicitly) perhaps his coolness was understandable. Crabb Robinson reported Wordsworth's response to his erstwhile friend's prose masterpiece: 'The praise is extravagant and the censure inconsiderate.' And while the lectures had been successful, Wordsworth had managed to make even Coleridge's fluency sound like a kind of vice, commenting that the series 'was, indeed, to him no effort, since his thoughts as well as his words flow spontaneously. He talks as a bird sings, as if he could not help it.'

Coleridge's life in 1818 saw some political pamphletry (the cause of the moment was child labour), a revised and rearranged three-volume edition of *The Friend* (now with interlinking essays and a 'Treatise on Method') and two more winter lecture series (this time at the Crown and Anchor Tavern off London's Strand) on Shakespeare and philosophy. Amid all this were the letters, and the non-stop scribbling in the notebooks. This was not the schedule of an idle man.

On the afternoon of 11th April 1819, Coleridge was walking on Hampstead Heath, near Highgate, with Joseph Henry Green, a surgeon friend of his and Gillman's. As they walked they came across a young man Green had supervised at Guy's Hospital, now a promising new voice in poetry; the young poet, who knew Coleridge's work, asked permission to walk and talk with the two older men for a mile or two, and on they went. The young man was a 23-year-old John Keats, who described the meeting and the conversation in a letter to his brother George. (The mad racing mixture of topics the poets discussed is very Coleridge...)

I walked with him a[t] his alderman-after-dinner pace for near two miles I suppose in those two Miles he broached a thousand things – let me see if I can give you a list – Nightingales, Poetry – on Poetical sensation – Metaphysics – Different genera and species of Dreams – Nightmare – a dream accompanied ~~with~~ by a sense of touch – single and double touch – A dream related – First and second consciousness – the difference explained between Will and Volition – so m[an]y metaphysicians from a want of smoking the second consciousness – Monsters – the Kraken – Mermaids – southey believes in them – southeys belief too much diluted – A Ghost story – Good morning – I heard his voice as he came towards me – I heard it as he moved away – I had heard it all the interval – if it may be called so...

Coleridge, for his part, claimed to remember the meeting ('A loose, slack, not well-dressed youth met Mr Green and myself...') for a particular sense of doom he felt in the young man's handshake:

After he had left us a little way, he came back and said: 'Let me carry away the memory, Coleridge, of having pressed your hand!' – 'There is death in that hand,' I said to Green when Keats was gone; yet this was, I believe, before the consumption showed itself distinctly...

The month of the now legendary Keats walk brought Coleridge some excellent news. His son Hartley was awarded a probationary fellowship at Oriel College, Oxford (he had been a student at Oxford, too). To Coleridge – who, it should be remembered, had never managed to take his own university degree – this was a matter of immense pride. He had been worried about Hartley, but now it was all going to be fine.

It would not last. A year later the college announced that they did not intend to renew the fellowship (citing the young man's unruly, drunken, inappropriate comportment). Hugely distressed, Coleridge tried everything to get the decision reversed, writing to the provost himself, compiling a dossier of character references for his son from the great and the good of his acquaintance (the poet laureate Southey, Walter Scott, William Wordsworth), but all to no avail. Troubles with Hartley at Oxford would be followed by troubles with Derwent at Cambridge; while he was not as wayward as his elder brother, he was apparently mixing in bad company (with people like the future poet-historian Thomas Babington Macaulay); it's just as well that these days daughter Sara was a delight to her old father (though he had doubts about her choice of fiancé…).

Meanwhile that other Sara, Sara Hutchinson – Asra – was not quite out of Coleridge's life either, even now. When they met in 1822, she treated him with kindness. The last line of 'The Pang More Sharp Than All', a poem begun many years earlier but to which Coleridge returned around now, may (so John Beer has suggested) be read as a reference to this.

I

He too has flitted from his secret nest,
Hope's last and dearest child without a name! –
Has flitted from me, like the warmthless flame,
That makes false promise of a place of rest

To the tired Pilgrim's still believing mind; –
Or like some Elfin Knight in kingly court,
Who having won all guerdons in his sport,
Glides out of view, and whither none can find!

II

Yes! he hath flitted from me – with what aim,
Or why, I know not! 'Twas a home of bliss,
And he was innocent, as the pretty shame
Of babe, that tempts and shuns the menaced kiss,
From its twy-cluster'd hiding place of snow!
Pure as the babe, I ween, and all aglow
As the dear hopes, that swell the mother's breast –
Her eyes down gazing o'er her claspéd charge; –
Yet gay as that twice happy father's kiss,
That well might glance aside, yet never miss,
Where the sweet mark emboss'd so sweet a targe –
Twice wretched he who hath been doubly blest!

III

Like a loose blossom on a gusty night
He flitted from me – and has left behind
(As if to them his faith he ne'er did plight)
Of either sex and answerable mind
Two playmates, twin-births of his foster-dame: –
The one a steady lad (Esteem he hight)
And Kindness is the gentler sister's name.
Dim likeness now, though fair she be and good,
Of that bright Boy who hath us all forsook; –
But in his full-eyed aspect when she stood,
And while her face reflected every look,
And in reflection kindled – she became
So like Him, that almost she seem'd the same!

Ah! he is gone, and yet will not depart! –
Is with me still, yet I from him exiled!
For still there lives within my secret heart
The magic image of the magic Child,
Which there he made up-grow by his strong art,
As in that crystal orb – wise Merlin's feat, –
The wondrous 'World of Glass,' wherein inisled
All long'd-for things their beings did repeat; –
And there he left it, like a Sylph beguiled,
To live and yearn and languish incomplete!

V

Can wit of man a heavier grief reveal?
Can sharper pang from hate or scorn arise? –
Yes! one more sharp there is that deeper lies,
Which fond Esteem but mocks when he would heal.
Yet neither scorn nor hate did it devise,
But sad compassion and atoning zeal!
One pang more blighting-keen than hope betray'd!
And this it is my woeful hap to feel,
When, at her Brother's hest, the twin-born Maid
With face averted and unsteady eyes,
Her truant playmate's faded robe puts on;
And inly shrinking from her own disguise
Enacts the faery Boy that's lost and gone.
O worse than all! O pang all pangs above
Is Kindness counterfeiting absent Love!

In September 1823 Coleridge completed 'Youth and Age', which looks back from his 51-year-old self to the days of his twenties in the Quantocks, in wistful mood.

Youth and Age

Verse, a breeze mid blossoms straying,
Where Hope clung feeding, like a bee –
Both were mine! Life went a-maying
    With Nature, Hope, and Poesy,
        When I was young!

When I was young? – Ah, woeful When!
Ah! for the change 'twixt Now and Then!
This breathing house not built with hands,
This body that does me grievous wrong,
O'er aery cliffs and glittering sands,
How lightly then it flashed along: –
Like those trim skiffs, unknown of yore,
On winding lakes and rivers wide,
That ask no aid of sail or oar,
That fear no spite of wind or tide!
Nought cared this body for wind or weather
When Youth and I lived in't together.

Flowers are lovely; Love is flower-like;
Friendship is a sheltering tree;
O! the joys, that came down shower-like,
Of Friendship, Love, and Liberty,
        Ere I was old!

Ere I was old? Ah woful Ere,
Which tells me, Youth's no longer here!
O Youth! for years so many and sweet
'Tis known, that Thou and I were one,
I'll think it but a fond conceit –
It cannot be that Thou art gone!
Thy vesper-bell hath not yet toll'd: –
And thou wert aye a masker bold!

What strange disguise hast now put on,
To make believe, that thou art gone?
I see these locks in silvery slips,
This drooping gait, this altered size:
But Spring-tide blossoms on thy lips,
And tears take sunshine from thine eyes!
Life is but thought: so think I will
That Youth and I are house-mates still.

Dew-drops are the gems of morning,
But the tears of mournful eve!
Where no hope is, life's a warning
That only serves to make us grieve,
*   When we are old:*

That only serves to make us grieve
With oft and tedious taking-leave,
Like some poor nigh-related guest,
That may not rudely be dismist;
Yet hath outstayed his welcome while,
And tells the jest without the smile.

Leigh Hunt wrote of 'Youth and Age', 'This is one of the most perfect poems, for style, feeling, and everything, that ever were written.'

In February 1825, ever wavering between a kind of resigned contentment and extreme anxieties about his abilities, Coleridge wrote this poem (populated with bees again), filled with doubts about his own self-worth:

Work without Hope

All Nature seems at work. Slugs leave their lair –
The bees are stirring – birds are on the wing –
And Winter slumbering in the open air,
Wears on his smiling face a dream of Spring!
And I, the while, the sole unbusy thing,
Nor honey make, nor pair, nor build, nor sing.

Yet well I ken the banks where amaranths blow,
Have traced the fount whence streams of nectar flow.
Bloom, O ye amaranths! bloom for whom ye may,
For me ye bloom not! Glide, rich streams, away!
With lips unbrightened, wreathless brow, I stroll:
And would you learn the spells that drowse my soul?
Work without Hope draws nectar in a sieve,
And Hope without an object cannot live.

Through all this Coleridge continued to work on his religious interests, especially on his *Aids to Reflection*, a work based on his appreciation of the seventeenth-century Anglican Archbishop Leighton (who had been important to him at the time of his West Country spiritual crisis). *Aids to Reflection* was a religious-philosophical treatise, which emphasised the importance of Christianity as a religion of 'personal revelation', and notable in part for its development of the distinction (after Kant's distinguishing of *Verstand* and *Vernunft*, also introduced by Coleridge in *The Friend*) of 'Reason' ('fixed') as distinct from 'Understanding' ('discursive'). The publication of *Aids to Reflection* in 1825 was (atypically in Coleridge's world) quite well received, which was excellent for morale. It would be one of the pillars on which Coleridge's reputation as a keen theological mind would rest. So too would another work occupying him at this time, *Confessions of a Inquiring Spirit*, which presents Coleridge's ideas of Biblical scholarship ('Letters on the

Inspiration of the Scriptures'), and which would not appear until after his death.

Alongside the theology was a slow-burn work on logic – *Logosophia* – that was to be his '*Opus maximum*', but which would never see publication.

Following further efforts towards an expanded edition of his poetical works in the spring of 1828, Coleridge spent some weeks travelling in Europe – his first trip abroad in years – going down the Rhine with Wordsworth and his daughter, Dora. William Wordsworth and Samuel Taylor Coleridge, two grumpy old men, tentatively restoring a lost friendship, travelling and grumbling about each other as they went; Germany, Holland, and home.

Cologne

In Köhln, a town of monks and bones,
And pavements fang'd with murderous stones
And rags, and hags, and hideous wenches;
I counted two and seventy stenches,
All well defined, and several stinks!
Ye Nymphs that reign o'er sewers and sinks,
The river Rhine, it is well known,
Doth wash your city of Cologne;
But tell me, Nymphs, what power divine
Shall henceforth wash the river Rhine?

The Netherlands
(a fragment)

Water and windmills, greenness, Islets green; –
Willows whose Trunks beside the shadows stood
Of their own higher half, and willowy swamp: –

> *Farmhouses that at anchor seem'd – in the inland sky*
> *The fog-transfixing Spires –*
> *Water, wide water, greenness and green banks,*
> *And water seen –*

In 1830 Coleridge published a monograph responding to major ongoing national debates about religion in which he proposed the establishment of a 'clerisy' class of educated people between lay and clergy; it was called 'On the Constitution of Church and State', and it would influence major Victorian theological thinkers; it would be the last major piece of work of Coleridge's lifetime.

Things were quieter for the final years. Domestic life with the Gillmans, visits from old and new friends, the occasional excursion (he managed a trip to Cambridge in 1833, where he met Michael Faraday), and the ongoing – seemingly un-winnable – battle to curb his addiction. The spring of 1832 saw a break of a few weeks in his use of the drug, but we only have his word for it.

In 1833, Coleridge wrote this, his 'Epitaph':

> *Stop, Christian passer-by! Stop, child of God,*
> *And read, with gentle breast. Beneath this sod*
> *A poet lies, or that which once seem'd he.*
> *O, lift one thought in prayer for S. T. C.;*
> *That he who many a year with toil of breath*
> *Found death in life, may here find life in death!*
> *Mercy for praise – to be forgiven for fame*
> *He ask'd, and hoped, through Christ. Do thou the same!*

The desirable 'life in death' sought here is quite different from the nightmare of that name he had created for his Mariner…

Coleridge was very sick now. He had heart trouble, and lung trouble – the years of opium had done damage he would never be able to repair. He hadn't stopped working, even now – even in the early months of 1834 he was working on a new edition of his poetical works – though the ill health made it increasingly difficult.

In July he deteriorated rapidly. On the 24th he mused, 'I could even be witty…', and soon afterwards slipped into a coma. At half past six the next morning he died. The difficult journey was over. The kind-hearted Charles Lamb, who had been his travelling companion for so many stormy years, wrote a tribute. Lamb would die too before the year was out.

When I heard of the death of Coleridge, it was without grief. It seemed to me he had long been on the confines of the next world, – that he had a hunger for eternity. I grieved then that I could not grieve. But since, I feel how great a part he was of me. His great and dear spirit haunts me. I cannot think a thought, I cannot make a criticism on men and books, without an ineffectual turning and reference to him. He was the proof and touchstone of all my cogitations… Never saw I his likeness, nor probably the world can see again.

O sleep! It is a gentle thing…

An autopsy was carried out on the body – Coleridge, curious even after death, had specifically requested that he should have one – and found his heart greatly enlarged. On 2nd August the body was buried at Old Highgate Chapel. In 1931 a plaque marking his birthplace was placed on the south wall of the churchyard at Ottery St Mary. In June 1961, following the building of the new Highgate School chapel, the bodies of Coleridge and his wife and daughter would be moved over to St Michael's church in Highgate, opposite the old Gillman house on the Grove, where they lie in the crypt today.

T.S. Eliot would call Coleridge 'perhaps the greatest of English critics'. Leigh Hunt, who had been a huge admirer of Coleridge's poetry, wrote:

> Oh! It is too late now; and habit and self-love blinded me at the time, and I did not know (much as I admired him) how great a poet lived in that grove at Highgate; or I would have cultivated its walks more, as I might have done, and endeavoured to return him, with my gratitude, a small portion of the delight his verses have given me.

Unseen work from Coleridge continued to appear after his death; apart from *Inquiring Spirit* there would be the first edition of *Table Talk*, a tantalising record of something that couldn't really ever be captured adequately – this which was published in 1835, reprinted the following year; but a great deal remained unpublished, with so many of his ambitious projects never close to completion (several of them barely begun). That his promise was greater than those achievements he actually managed to complete is beyond dispute, and that is what is often remembered in appraisals of his work; however, by any standards but his own he would still be judged incredibly prolific (his collected works run to twenty-three volumes, not including the letters and Note-books!), and his legacy hugely influential in many areas.

His late prose influenced the young intellectuals of early Victorian years, his poetry – and through his influence, Wordsworth's – affected countless other poets and writers (from his contemporaries to those writing today). In large part this was because of the *Lyrical Ballads*, of course, but also through much other work (so for a fan like the Gothically inclined Edgar Allen Poe, for example, one might suggest an affinity to 'Christabel' as much as to the 'Mariner').

Stevie Smith wrote a poem called 'Thoughts About the Person from Porlock' in which she professes envy that Coleridge had such a good excuse for not getting his poem finished. Coleridge's friendship with Wordsworth is the subject of countless books, and films too – he's played by Linus Roache in *Pandemonium*, whose closing credits see him riding the London Eye. In Douglas Adams's *Dirk Gently's Holistic Detective Agency* the legacy of Coleridge is dragged into a hilarious Cambridge-set mystery story involving a little bit of time-travel and an Electric Monk.

Coleridge was, wrote Leigh Hunt, 'the finest dreamer, the most eloquent talker, and the most original thinker of his day'. For John Stuart Mill, he was (with Jeremy Bentham) simply one of the two great minds of the age.

A plagiarist and a drug addict, a negligent husband tortured by an enduring love for the wrong woman, Coleridge's was not a life that seemed to be filled with triumphs. But in posterity – with the biographical upsets long faded – it is much easier to appreciate the many, varied glories of his surviving work. Coleridge was an important philosopher and religious thinker; he was a ground-breaking literary critic; and he was one of the creators of the *Lyrical Ballads*, which proposed and embodied a radical new voice for poetry.

But it's no surprise that it was as a poet (especially of just a certain small number of poems) that he would be chiefly remembered. The plaque to his memory donated by the Gillmans celebrated a 'poet, philosopher and theologian', in that order – even though in the years he lived with them he was hardly a poet at all, and his poetry was on the whole little valued in his lifetime. But his philosophy and theology would drift out of fashion; to us, today, he is rightly most celebrated as the author (in just a few short, miraculous years) of conversation poems 'Frost at Midnight', 'This Lime-Tree Bower...', 'The Nightingale' and 'Dejection'; of 'Kubla Khan', 'Christabel' and, of course, the third in that supernatural trio, the ballad called 'The Rime of the Ancient Mariner'.

The Rime of the Ancient Mariner
In Seven Parts

PART I

It is an ancient Mariner,
And he stoppeth one of three.
'By thy long grey beard and glittering eye,
Now wherefore stopp'st thou me?

The Bridegroom's doors are opened wide,
And I am next of kin;
The guests are met, the feast is set:
May'st hear the merry din.'

He holds him with his skinny hand,
'There was a ship,' quoth he.
'Hold off! unhand me, grey-beard loon!'
Eftsoons his hand dropt he.

He holds him with his glittering eye –
The Wedding-Guest stood still,
And listens like a three years' child:
The Mariner hath his will.

The Wedding-Guest sat on a stone:
He cannot choose but hear;
And thus spake on that ancient man,
The bright-eyed Mariner.

'The ship was cheered, the harbour cleared,
Merrily did we drop
Below the kirk, below the hill,
Below the lighthouse top.

The Sun came up upon the left,
Out of the sea came he!
And he shone bright, and on the right
Went down into the sea.

Higher and higher every day,
Till over the mast at noon – '
The Wedding-Guest here beat his breast,
For he heard the loud bassoon.

The bride hath paced into the hall,
Red as a rose is she;
Nodding their heads before her goes
The merry minstrelsy.

The Wedding-Guest he beat his breast,
Yet he cannot choose but hear;
And thus spake on that ancient man,
The bright-eyed Mariner.

'And now the STORM-BLAST came, and he
Was tyrannous and strong:
He struck with his o'ertaking wings,
And chased us south along.

With sloping masts and dipping prow,
As who pursued with yell and blow
Still treads the shadow of his foe,
And forward bends his head,
The ship drove fast, loud roared the blast,
And southward aye we fled.

And now there came both mist and snow,
And it grew wondrous cold:
And ice, mast-high, came floating by,
As green as emerald.

And through the drifts the snowy clifts
Did send a dismal sheen:
Nor shapes of men nor beasts we ken –
The ice was all between.

The ice was here, the ice was there,
The ice was all around:
It cracked and growled, and roared and howled,
Like noises in a swound!

At length did cross an Albatross,
Thorough the fog it came;
As if it had been a Christian soul,
We hailed it in God's name.

It ate the food it ne'er had eat,
And round and round it flew.
The ice did split with a thunder-fit;
The helmsman steered us through!

And a good south wind sprung up behind;
The Albatross did follow,
And every day, for food or play,
Came to the Mariner's hollo!

In mist or cloud, on mast or shroud,
It perched for vespers nine;
Whiles all the night, through fog-smoke white,
Glimmered the white Moon-shine.'

'God save thee, ancient Mariner!
From the fiends, that plague thee thus! –
Why look'st thou so?' – 'With my cross-bow
I shot the ALBATROSS.'

PART II

The Sun now rose upon the right:
Out of the sea came he,
Still hid in mist, and on the left
Went down into the sea.

And the good south wind still blew behind,
But no sweet bird did follow,
Nor any day for food or play
Came to the mariners' hollo!

And I had done a hellish thing,
And it would work 'em woe:
For all averred, I had killed the bird
That made the breeze to blow.
Ah wretch! said they, the bird to slay,
That made the breeze to blow!

Nor dim nor red like God's own head,
The glorious Sun uprist:
Then all averred, I had killed the bird
That brought the fog and mist.
'Twas right, said they, such birds to slay,
That bring the fog and mist.

The fair breeze blew, the white foam flew,
The furrow followed free;
We were the first that ever burst
Into that silent sea.

Down dropt the breeze, the sails dropt down,
'Twas sad as sad could be;
And we did speak only to break
The silence of the sea!

All in a hot and copper sky,
The bloody Sun, at noon,
Right up above the mast did stand,
No bigger than the Moon.

Day after day, day after day,
We stuck, nor breath nor motion;
As idle as a painted ship
Upon a painted ocean.

Water, water, every where,
And all the boards did shrink;
Water, water, every where,
Nor any drop to drink.

The very deep did rot: O Christ!
That ever this should be!
Yea, slimy things did crawl with legs
Upon the slimy sea.

About, about, in reel and rout
The death-fires danced at night;
The water, like a witch's oils,
Burnt green, and blue and white.

And some in dreams assuréd were
Of the Spirit that plagued us so;
Nine fathom deep he had followed us
From the land of mist and snow.

And every tongue, through utter drought,
Was withered at the root;
We could not speak, no more than if
We had been choked with soot.

Ah! well a-day! what evil looks
Had I from old and young!
Instead of the cross, the Albatross
About my neck was hung.

Part III

There passed a weary time. Each throat
Was parched, and glazed each eye.
A weary time! a weary time!
How glazed each weary eye,
When looking westward, I beheld
A something in the sky.

At first it seemed a little speck,
And then it seemed a mist;
It moved and moved, and took at last
A certain shape, I wist.

A speck, a mist, a shape, I wist!
And still it neared and neared:
As if it dodged a water-sprite,
It plunged and tacked and veered.

With throats unslaked, with black lips baked,
We could nor laugh nor wail;
Through utter drought all dumb we stood!
I bit my arm, I sucked the blood,
And cried, A sail! a sail!

With throats unslaked, with black lips baked,
Agape they heard me call:
Gramercy! they for joy did grin
And all at once their breath drew in,
As they were drinking all.

See! see! (I cried) she tacks no more!
Hither to work us weal;
Without a breeze, without a tide,
She steadies with upright keel!

The western wave was all a-flame.
The day was well nigh done!
Almost upon the western wave
Rested the broad bright Sun;
When that strange shape drove suddenly
Betwixt us and the Sun.

And straight the Sun was flecked with bars,
(Heaven's Mother send us grace!)
As if through a dungeon-grate he peered
With broad and burning face.

Alas! (thought I, and my heart beat loud)
How fast she nears and nears!
Are those her sails that glance in the Sun,
Like restless gossameres?

Are those her ribs through which the Sun
Did peer, as through a grate?
And is that Woman all her crew?
Is that a DEATH? and are there two?
Is DEATH that woman's mate?

Her lips were red, her looks were free,
Her locks were yellow as gold:
Her skin was as white as leprosy,
The Night-mare LIFE-IN-DEATH was she,
Who thicks man's blood with cold.

The naked hulk alongside came,
And the twain were casting dice;
'The game is done! I've won! I've won!'
Quoth she, and whistles thrice.

The Sun's rim dips; the stars rush out:
At one stride comes the dark;
With far-heard whisper, o'er the sea,
Off shot the spectre-bark.

We listened and looked sideways up!
Fear at my heart, as at a cup,
My life-blood seemed to sip!
The stars were dim, and thick the night,
The steersman's face by his lamp gleamed white;
From the sails the dew did drip –
Till clomb above the eastern bar
The hornéd Moon, with one bright star
Within the nether tip.

One after one, by the star-dogged Moon,
Too quick for groan or sigh,
Each turned his face with a ghastly pang,
And cursed me with his eye.

Four times fifty living men,
(And I heard nor sigh nor groan)
With heavy thump, a lifeless lump,
They dropped down one by one.

The souls did from their bodies fly, –
They fled to bliss or woe!
And every soul, it passed me by,
Like the whizz of my cross-bow!

PART IV

'I fear thee, ancient Mariner!
I fear thy skinny hand!
And thou art long, and lank, and brown,
As is the ribbed sea-sand.

I fear thee and thy glittering eye,
And thy skinny hand, so brown.' –
Fear not, fear not, thou Wedding-Guest!
This body dropt not down.

Alone, alone, all, all alone,
Alone on a wide wide sea!
And never a saint took pity on
My soul in agony.

The many men, so beautiful!
And they all dead did lie:
And a thousand thousand slimy things
Lived on; and so did I.

I looked upon the rotting sea,
And drew my eyes away;
I looked upon the rotting deck,
And there the dead men lay

I looked to Heaven, and tried to pray;
But or ever a prayer had gusht,
A wicked whisper came, and made
My heart as dry as dust.

I closed my lids, and kept them close,
And the balls like pulses beat;
For the sky and the sea, and the sea and the sky
Lay like a load on my weary eye,
And the dead were at my feet.

The cold sweat melted from their limbs,
Nor rot nor reek did they:
The look with which they looked on me
Had never passed away.

An orphan's curse would drag to hell
A spirit from on high;
But oh! more horrible than that
Is the curse in a dead man's eye!
Seven days, seven nights I saw that curse,
And yet I could not die.

The moving Moon went up the sky,
And no where did abide:
Softly she was going up,
And a star or two beside –

Her beams bemocked the sultry main,
Like April hoar-frost spread;
But where the ship's huge shadow lay,
The charméd water burnt alway
A still and awful red.

Beyond the shadow of the ship,
I watched the water-snakes:
They moved in tracks of shining white
And when they reared, the elfish light
Fell off in hoary flakes.

Within the shadow of the ship
I watched their rich attire:
Blue, glossy green, and velvet black,
They coiled and swam; and every track
Was a flash of golden fire.

O happy living things! no tongue
Their beauty might declare:
A spring of love gushed from my heart,
And I blessed them unaware:
Sure my kind saint took pity on me,
And I blessed them unaware.

The self-same moment I could pray;
And from my neck so free
The Albatross fell off, and sank
Like lead into the sea.

PART V

Oh sleep! it is a gentle thing,
Beloved from pole to pole!
To Mary Queen the praise be given!
She sent the gentle sleep from Heaven,
That slid into my soul.

The silly buckets on the deck,
That had so long remained,
I dreamt that they were filled with dew;
And when I awoke, it rained.

My lips were wet, my throat was cold,
My garments all were dank;
Sure I had drunken in my dreams,
And still my body drank.

I moved, and could not feel my limbs:
I was so light – almost
I thought that I had died in sleep,
And was a blessèd ghost.

And soon I heard a roaring wind:
It did not come anear;
But with its sound it shook the sails,
That were so thin and sere.

The upper air burst into life!
And a hundred fire-flags sheen,
To and fro they were hurried about!
And to and fro, and in and out,
The wan stars danced between.

And the coming wind did roar more loud,
And the sails did sigh like sedge;
And the rain poured down from one black cloud;
The Moon was at its edge.

The thick black cloud was cleft, and still
The Moon was at its side:
Like waters shot from some high crag,
The lightning fell with never a jag,
A river steep and wide.

The loud wind never reached the ship,
Yet now the ship moved on!
Beneath the lightning and the Moon
The dead men gave a groan.

They groaned, they stirred, they all uprose,
Nor spake, nor moved their eyes;
It had been strange, even in a dream,
To have seen those dead men rise.

The helmsman steered, the ship moved on;
Yet never a breeze up-blew;
The mariners all 'gan work the ropes,
Where they were wont to do;
They raised their limbs like lifeless tools –
We were a ghastly crew.

The body of my brother's son
Stood by me, knee to knee:
The body and I pulled at one rope,
But he said nought to me.

'I fear thee, ancient Mariner!'
Be calm, thou Wedding-Guest!
'Twas not those souls that fled in pain,
Which to their corses came again,
But a troop of spirits blest:

For when it dawned – they dropped their arms,
And clustered round the mast;
Sweet sounds rose slowly through their mouths,
And from their bodies passed.

Around, around, flew each sweet sound,
Then darted to the Sun;
Slowly the sounds came back again,
Now mixed, now one by one.

Sometimes a-dropping from the sky
I heard the sky-lark sing;
Sometimes all little birds that are,
How they seemed to fill the sea and air
With their sweet jargoning!

And now 'twas like all instruments,
Now like a lonely flute;
And now it is an angel's song,
That makes the heavens be mute.

It ceased; yet still the sails made on
A pleasant noise till noon,
A noise like of a hidden brook
In the leafy month of June,
That to the sleeping woods all night
Singeth a quiet tune.

Till noon we quietly sailed on,
Yet never a breeze did breathe:
Slowly and smoothly went the Ship,
Moved onward from beneath.

Under the keel nine fathom deep,
From the land of mist and snow,
The spirit slid: and it was he
That made the ship to go.
The sails at noon left off their tune,
And the ship stood still also.

The Sun, right up above the mast,
Had fixed her to the ocean:
But in a minute she 'gan stir,
With a short uneasy motion –
Backwards and forwards half her length
With a short uneasy motion.

Then like a pawing horse let go,
She made a sudden bound:
It flung the blood into my head,
And I fell down in a swound.

How long in that same fit I lay,
I have not to declare;
But ere my living life returned,
I heard and in my soul discerned
Two voices in the air.

'Is it he?' quoth one, 'Is this the man?
By him who died on cross,
With his cruel bow he laid full low
The harmless Albatross.

The spirit who bideth by himself
In the land of mist and snow,
He loved the bird that loved the man
Who shot him with his bow.'

The other was a softer voice,
As soft as honey-dew:
Quoth he, 'The man hath penance done,
And penance more will do.'

Part VI

First Voice

'But tell me, tell me! speak again,
They soft response renewing –
What makes that ship drive on so fast?
What is the ocean doing?'

Second Voice

'Still as a slave before his lord,
The ocean hath no blast;
His great bright eye most silently
Up to the Moon is cast –

If he may know which way to go;
For she guides him smooth or grim.
See, brother, see! how graciously
She looketh down on him.'

First Voice

'But why drives on that ship so fast,
Without or wave or wind?'

Second Voice

'The air is cut away before,
And closes from behind.

Fly, brother, fly! more high, more high!
Or we shall be belated:
For slow and slow that ship will go,
When the Mariner's trance is abated.'

I woke, and we were sailing on
As in a gentle weather:
'Twas night, calm night, the moon was high;
The dead men stood together.

All stood together on the deck,
For a charnel-dungeon fitter:
All fixed on me their stony eyes,
That in the Moon did glitter.

The pang, the curse, with which they died,
Had never passed away:
I could not draw my eyes from theirs,
Nor turn them up to pray.

And now this spell was snapt: once more
I viewed the ocean green,
And looked far forth, yet little saw
Of what had else been seen –

Like one, that on a lonesome road
Doth walk in fear and dread,
And having once turned round walks on,
And turns no more his head;
Because he knows, a frightful fiend
Doth close behind him tread.

But soon there breathed a wind on me,
Nor sound nor motion made:
Its path was not upon the sea,
In ripple or in shade.

It raised my hair, it fanned my cheek
Like a meadow-gale of spring –
It mingled strangely with my fears,
Yet it felt like a welcoming.

Swiftly, swiftly flew the ship,
Yet she sailed softly too:
Sweetly, sweetly blew the breeze –
On me alone it blew.

Oh! dream of joy! is this indeed
The light-house top I see?
Is this the hill? is this the kirk?
Is this mine own countree?

We drifted o'er the harbour-bar,
And I with sobs did pray –
O let me be awake, my God!
Or let me sleep alway.

The harbour-bay was clear as glass,
So smoothly it was strewn!
And on the bay, the moonlight lay,
And the shadow of the Moon.

The rock shone bright, the kirk no less,
That stands above the rock:
The moonlight steeped in silentness
The steady weathercock.

And the bay was white with silent light,
Till rising from the same,
Full many shapes, that shadows were,
In crimson colours came.

A little distance from the prow
Those crimson shadows were:
I turned my eyes upon the deck –
Oh, Christ! what saw I there!

Each corse lay flat, lifeless and flat,
And, by the holy rood!
A man all light, a seraph-man,
On every corse there stood.

This seraph-band, each waved his hand:
It was a heavenly sight!
They stood as signals to the land,
Each one a lovely light;

This seraph-band, each waved his hand,
No voice did they impart –
No voice; but oh! the silence sank
Like music on my heart.

But soon I heard the dash of oars,
I heard the Pilot's cheer;
My head was turned perforce away
And I saw a boat appear.

The Pilot and the Pilot's boy,
I heard them coming fast:
Dear Lord in Heaven! it was a joy
The dead men could not blast.

I saw a third – I heard his voice:
It is the Hermit good!
He singeth loud his godly hymns
That he makes in the wood.
He'll shrieve my soul, he'll wash away
The Albatross's blood.

PART VII

This Hermit good lives in that wood
Which slopes down to the sea.
How loudly his sweet voice he rears!
He loves to talk with marineres
That come from a far countree.

He kneels at morn, and noon, and eve –
He hath a cushion plump:
It is the moss that wholly hides
The rotted old oak-stump.

The skiff-boat neared: I heard them talk,
'Why, this is strange, I trow!
Where are those lights so many and fair,
That signal made but now?'

'Strange, by my faith!' the Hermit said –
'And they answered not our cheer!
The planks looked warped! and see those sails,
How thin they are and sere!
I never saw aught like to them,
Unless perchance it were

Brown skeletons of leaves that lag
My forest-brook along;
When the ivy-tod is heavy with snow,
And the owlet whoops to the wolf below,
That eats the she-wolf's young.'

'Dear Lord! it hath a fiendish look –
(The Pilot made reply)
I am a-feared' – 'Push on, push on!'
Said the Hermit cheerily.

The boat came closer to the ship,
But I nor spake nor stirred;
The boat came close beneath the ship,
And straight a sound was heard.

Under the water it rumbled on,
Still louder and more dead:
It reached the ship, it split the bay;
The ship went down like lead.

Stunned by that loud and dreadful sound,
Which sky and ocean smote,
Like one that hath been seven days drowned
My body lay afloat;
But swift as dreams, myself I found
Within the Pilot's boat.

Upon the whirl, where sank the ship,
The boat spun round and round;
And all was still, save that the hill
Was telling of the sound.

I moved my lips – the Pilot shrieked
And fell down in a fit;
The holy Hermit raised his eyes,
And prayed where he did sit.

I took the oars: the Pilot's boy,
Who now doth crazy go,
Laughed loud and long, and all the while
His eyes went to and fro.
'Ha! ha!' quoth he, 'full plain I see,
The Devil knows how to row.'

And now, all in my own countree,
I stood on the firm land!
The Hermit stepped forth from the boat,
And scarcely he could stand.

'O shrieve me, shrieve me, holy man!'
The Hermit crossed his brow.
'Say quick,' quoth he, 'I bid thee say –
What manner of man art thou?'

Forthwith this frame of mine was wrenched
With a woful agony,
Which forced me to begin my tale;
And then it left me free.

Since then, at an uncertain hour,
That agony returns:
And till my ghastly tale is told,
This heart within me burns.

I pass, like night, from land to land;
I have strange power of speech;
That moment that his face I see,
I know the man that must hear me:
To him my tale I teach.

What loud uproar bursts from that door!
The wedding-guests are there:
But in the garden-bower the bride
And bride-maids singing are:
And hark the little vesper bell,
Which biddeth me to prayer!

O Wedding-Guest! this soul hath been
Alone on a wide wide sea:
So lonely 'twas, that God himself
Scarce seeméd there to be.

O sweeter than the marriage-feast,
'Tis sweeter far to me,
To walk together to the kirk
With a goodly company! –

To walk together to the kirk,
And all together pray,
While each to his great Father bends,
Old men, and babes, and loving friends
And youths and maidens gay!

Farewell, farewell! but this I tell
To thee, thou Wedding-Guest!
He prayeth well, who loveth well
Both man and bird and beast.

He prayeth best, who loveth best
All things both great and small;
For the dear God who loveth us,
He made and loveth all.

The Mariner, whose eye is bright,
Whose beard with age is hoar,
Is gone: and now the Wedding-Guest
Turned from the bridegroom's door.

He went like one that hath been stunned,
And is of sense forlorn:
A sadder and a wiser man
He rose the morrow morn.

List of works

The dates given in brackets correspond to the (sometimes approximate) date of composition.

The text of the poems reproduced in this book has been taken from Ernest Hartley Coleridge's edition of 1912.

Further reading

The works, first of all. The poems in this volume are given as they appear in Ernest Hartley Coleridge's 1912 edition, which is in turn based on the 1834 three-volume Pickering edition (the last published in the poet's lifetime). The Notebooks are quoted from the definitive Kathleen Coburn edition (the first volume of which appeared in 1957); the letters from the 1895 Ernest Hartley Coleridge edition; and *Biographia Literaria* from the 1975 Everyman re-edition by George Watson.

Condensing a life longer than sixty years and a personality as unique as Coleridge's into a volume of this size (especially when you have to leave room for 'The Ancient Mariner') means this is really only a sprint through the basic facts. (And what, no 'Christabel'? You actually *cut* 'Fears in Solitude'?!) Coleridge deserves a rich, leisurely portrait, he deserves being read in a magnificent, rich, sympathetic, teeming biography that is the only way to do him justice. And there's no point suggesting that there's any doubt about this at all: if you want to read a biography of Coleridge, you read Richard Holmes. The first volume, *Coleridge: Early Visions*, which takes the story up to the poet's departure for Malta, is not only the best book about Coleridge I know, but my favourite biography, by anyone, of anyone. And the second volume, *Coleridge: Darker Reflections*, is a worthy companion-piece to it. Alongside these, any other book on this subject feels very pale, very scrawny and bloodless indeed. There are other good ones, of course – I like Rosemary Ashton's full life very much, or Alethea Hayter's *A Voyage in Vain* which looks day-by-day at the boat trip to Malta – but really none that can compare to the Holmes double.

A couple of other oddities worth a mention, though: *The Damaged Archangel* by Norman Fruman takes a critical (in both senses) look at the plagiarism/borrowing, a habit of Coleridge's which damaged his reputation right through the nineteenth century. And anyone taken by the poetry should dive into *The Road to Xanadu*, John Livingstone Lowes's unique investigations into the origins of the 'Mariner' and 'Kubla Khan' based on an exploration of Coleridge's own reading. It's pretty odd.

Acknowledgments

I've been reading Coleridge for a long time, and many people have contributed to that process of discovery, and to the production of this book, often without realising it. Thanks first, then, to Dr Fred Parker at the English faculty in Cambridge, who quite possibly won't remember but very many years ago was the brilliant supervisor of a dissertation on the Coleridge Notebooks. Later I spent a year in Germany researching Coleridge and Wordsworth's winter there, thanks to a fellowship from the Alfred Toepfer Foundation, and A.S. Byatt who nominated me for it, and part of my research from that year has been siphoned into this book. Clearly I was always meant to write a book about Coleridge sometime, and I have to thank Hesperus Press for allowing me to do it, at last. Thanks also to Alexis Ashley-Korner, who shared a couple of good conversations about the poet just as I was getting started thinking about the book, which reminded me how interesting it all was. Margaret Drabble is my own person from Porlock (but in a good way) – from her house over the last years I've visited Coleridge Cottage, walked the path to Culbone Church, and got to know my way around many of the places Coleridge knew and loved best. My friends Iannis and Anna hosted me in Freiburg while I was writing my notes; Jeronimé and Scott allowed me to spend a few wonderful days staying at Greta Hall itself (parts of which are now available to rent out – a much recommended opportunity – more about that at www.gretahall.net), and Ileana and Denis kept me company while I was there, made delicious chicken soup and taught me the word 'anhedonia'. Kay Langley-May showed me St Michael's Church in Highgate, kindly allowing me into the unusual crypt too (and is going to read the 'Mariner' again now); and Mary Howman bought me drinks while I was in the area and patiently allowed me to talk to her about my plans for this book. Everyone in Rio, where this book was completed, for endless printing, feeding, etc. And Abigail Anderson – my most constant collaborator, I think – spent a morning with me punctuating Coleridge poems.

My relationship with Coleridge began when I was a teenager, when my mother gave me 'The Ancient Mariner' to read. This book is dedicated to her.

Biographical note

Daniel Hahn is a writer, editor and translator. Among other books, he is the author of *The Tower Menagerie*; the translator of four novels by Angolan novelist José Eduardo Agualusa (winning him the 2007 Independent Foreign Fiction Prize); and the editor of a number of reference books including *The Oxford Guide to Literary Britain and Ireland* (with Nicholas Robins), which he only now realises is missing an enormously famous Coleridge anecdote. He grew up in London, living for many years just round the corner from Coleridge's Highgate house, and subsequently wrote his undergraduate dissertation on Coleridge's Notebooks and dreams.